WHY

SCRIPTURAL ANSWERS
TO CHRISTIAN BELIEFS

ALLEN DOMELLE

For more copies:

Allen Domelle Ministries
PO Box 1595
Bethany, OK 73008
903.746.9632

TABLE OF CONTENTS

CHAPTER ONE

APPEARANCE

Appearance matters, because it identifies you. I was talking with a lady who visited my church who was trying to get across to her teenage boy, who had some run-ins with the law, that his identity mattered. She knew that his hair and clothing mattered to the police because it identified him with a group of people.

Whether or not we like it, people profile one another by how they are dressed. What we call profiling is God's way of helping us to protect ourselves. Everyone profiles. Parents often tell their children that they can't associate with a group of people because they are bad. Those parents are profiling that group, in many cases, because of the way they are dressed.

For many years, my wife and I have had Rottweilers as our pets. I love my dogs, and they are very good dogs; however, I have found that many people cross the street when I am walking them because they think they are mean dogs. What are they doing? They are profiling my dogs. Does this make them bad people? No, it does not, because it is merely a part of our human makeup to want to protect ourselves.

In 1 Kings 10:1-7, the queen of Sheba heard about the wisdom and riches of Solomon. Because of her disbelief in all the good that she heard, she came to prove Solomon with hard questions. However, when she came and saw everything, she couldn't believe what she saw. 1 Kings 10:4-5, says, *"And when the queen of Sheba had seen all Solomon's wisdom, and the house that he had built, And the meat of his table, and the sitting of his servants, and the attendance of his ministers, and their apparel, and his cupbearers, and his ascent by which he went up unto the house of the LORD; there was no more spirit in her."* I want you to notice that one of the things that changed the mind of this queen concerning Solomon was the *"apparel"* of the servants. Imagine if the servants were unkempt in their dress; do you think she would have been impressed? The appearance of these servants did matter, and it did change the way she treated Solomon.

Your appearance matters. It matters because people look at your appearance and make a judgment about you. It matters because you behave according to your appearance. If you dress sloppily, you are most likely going to be a bit unruly and lazy. If you dress right, you tend to behave right and carry yourself better. Your appearance matters because you belong to God and people are watching you. Let's look at what the Scriptures teach about the importance of keeping a right appearance.

1. You should dress right because your body is the temple of the Holy Ghost.

1 Corinthians 6:19 says, *"What? know ye not that your body is the temple of the Holy Ghost which is in you, which ye have of God, and ye are not your own?"* The clothes you wear should not represent the world's styles. The clothes you wear should be a good representation of the Holy Ghost who lives inside of you. Too many people are concerned with keeping up with the world's styles, and many times the world's styles don't represent how the LORD would want you to dress. I am not saying you have to dress like your grandparents, but I am saying your clothing styles should be pleasing to the Holy Ghost. I don't believe tight-fitting pants on men, revealing dresses on women, raggedy clothing that has holes all through them is a good representation of the Holy Ghost. Keep in mind that what you wear should show the

world that you have the Holy Ghost living inside of you.

2. You should dress your best because you are commanded to do your best.

Ecclesiastes 9:10 says, *"Whatsoever thy hand findeth to do, do it with thy might..."* A believer should always be dressed sharply because they are commanded to be their best. In other words, it is good for the believer to iron their clothes, and to keep their clothing clean. You are to do your best, and wrinkled and dirty clothing is not your best. You may not be able to afford nicer clothing, but you can always take care of the clothing you wear.

3. You should dress sharp because you represent God.

1 Corinthians 4:9 says, *"For I think that God hath set forth us the apostles last, as it were appointed to death: for we are made a*

spectacle unto the world, and to angels, and to men." The word *"spectacle"* is saying that you are a screen to the world. In other words, the world should look at you and see that the way you dress represents God. You don't have a right to dress the way you want to because you belong to God. You should dress according to how God would want you to dress.

4. You should dress right because God is watching how you dress.

1 Corinthians 4:9 shows that the angels are watching. In other words, Heaven is looking down and seeing how you dress. God is interested in your appearance, and you should dress in such a manner that you wouldn't be ashamed if He saw you on the street in what you are wearing. I believe more believers would dress better and more sharply if they recognized that God is looking down from Heaven at their appearance.

5. You should dress according to the activity.

Ecclesiastes 3:1 says, *"To every thing there is a season, and a time to every purpose under the heaven:"* There are right ways and wrong ways to dress for activities. The believer should learn how to dress according to the activity. For instance, you wouldn't dig ditches in a suit and tie because that is not dressing accordingly. Likewise, the believer should dress accordingly when they go to church. You should go to church in church clothes, not work clothes, shorts, or casual wear. I believe it is right for men to at least wear a shirt and tie when they go to church, and for ladies to always wear a dress when they go to church. Your appearance in church affects your attentiveness to the preaching, and it impacts the visitors who are visiting your church. They should be able to tell by your appearance that church is important to you.

6. You should dress according to the example of the church leaders.

1 Corinthians 11:1 says, *"Be ye followers of me, even as I also am of Christ."* As long as Paul followed Christ, he admonished the Corinthian believers to follow him. You can learn how a believer should dress by looking at your pastor and his wife. Though they are not God, they are a good representation of how you should dress. This also means that every church leader has a huge responsibility to dress according to how God would want them to dress, and not according to how they want to dress. If you have questions about how you should dress for church, look at your church leaders and follow their example.

7. You should dress as if the LORD is coming today.

Matthew 24:42 says, *"Watch therefore: for ye know not what hour your Lord doth come."*

My friend, Jesus is coming soon, and you should dress in a manner in which you would want Him to find you. Would you want the LORD to find you how you have dressed lately? If not, you need to change how you dress and dress so that He would find you dressed appropriately, and in a sharp manner.

CHAPTER TWO

ABORTION

One of the most controversial subjects in society today is the topic of abortion. Many believe that abortion is a woman's choice, but others believe that life begins at conception and that abortion is murder. The best way to settle this argument is to go to the Scriptures to find out what they say about whether abortion is a woman's prerogative or if it is murder.

Abortion is defined as the deliberate termination of a human pregnancy. Though some would like to accept this as a good definition, this definition is not scriptural. The proper definition of abortion is that it is the deliberate termination of human life. In other words, abortion is murder. Isaiah 44:24 says, *"Thus saith the LORD, thy redeemer, and he that formed thee from the womb, I am the*

LORD *that maketh all things; that stretcheth forth the heavens alone; that spreadeth abroad the earth by myself;"* If the LORD forms us in the womb, that means that there is life at conception. (From this point forward, I will address abortion as murder.) Let me share with you what the Scriptures say about abortion being murder.

1. Just because man legalizes murder doesn't make it right.

Romans 3:4 says, *"...let God be true, but every man a liar;..."* The Scriptures are clear that when man's decisions contradict God's Word, God's Word is right and man's decision is wrong. Just because the Supreme Court legalized murder in the Roe v Wade case in 1973, doesn't make it right. God's Word always takes authority over the Supreme Court decisions. The justices may deem that there is no life at conception, but that doesn't change the fact that life begins at conception.

11

2. God defines a woman who is pregnant as "with child."

Genesis 16:11 says, *"And the angel of the LORD said unto her, Behold, thou art with child, and shalt bear a son..."* Twenty-six times in the Scriptures, God uses the phrase *"with child"* to describe a woman who is pregnant. Being pregnant does not mean there is life, but being with child does. The whole reason our society has debated whether there is life at conception is because we have forsaken God's terminology of defining a woman with child.

3. Life happenings occur in the womb.

When talking about John the Baptist, Luke 1:15 says, *"For he shall be great in the sight of the Lord, and shall drink neither wine nor strong drink; and he shall be filled with the Holy Ghost, even from his mother's womb."* God continues in Luke 1:41 by saying, *"...the babe leaped in her womb..."* The Holy Spirit does not fill matter, but He does fill a life. Likewise, a dead piece of flesh can't leap; only something with life can leap. Therefore, it is easy to see that there is life in the womb.

4. God says that murder is a sin.

Part of the Ten Commandments teaches in Exodus 20:13, *"Thou shalt not kill."* If there is life at conception and in the womb, it means that taking that life is murder. Therefore, it is murder and against God's Word to take the life of another human being, even though that life is in the womb.

5. God calls abortion an abomination.

God calls murder an abomination. Abomination means that it is an outrage and disgusting to someone. Proverbs 6:16-17 says, *"These six things doth the LORD hate: yea, seven are an abomination unto him: A proud look, a lying tongue, and hands that shed*

13

innocent blood," Killing a baby in the womb is shedding innocent blood. That baby in the womb is life, and God detests it when anyone takes the life of a baby.

6. Abortion is always coupled with evil.

Murdering babies is not something new. When reading God's Word, you find that people in the past were as guilty as many are today with killing babies. The first person that comes to mind is Pharaoh. When Pharaoh saw the growth of the Jews, he became so concerned that they would overtake the Egyptians that he made a decree that the midwives were to kill any male baby that was born. Exodus 1:16 says, *"And he said, When ye do the office of a midwife to the Hebrew women, and see them upon the stools; if it be a son, then ye shall kill him: but if it be a daughter, then she shall live."* This was an evil plot by Pharaoh to kill every male baby that was born to the Israelites.

Herod also made the same tragic decision in Matthew 2:16, *"Then Herod, when he saw that he was mocked of the wise men, was exceeding wroth, and sent forth, and slew all the children that were in Bethlehem, and in all the coasts thereof, from two years old and under, according to the time which he had diligently enquired of the wise men."* Herod was fearful of his throne being taken by Jesus; therefore, a decree was made to kill all babies two years of age and below.

Another occurrence of children being murdered is found in 2 Kings 23:10 where it says, *"And he defiled Topheth, which is in the valley of the children of Hinnom, that no man might make his son or his daughter to pass through the fire to Molech."* These people had become so calloused about life that they threw their babies into the fire to please Molech. Only an evil heart would make these decisions to kill these innocent babies, and the hearts of politicians, doctors, and people who are willing to kill a child in the womb are very evil.

7. Abortion has always been done because someone was inconvenienced.

In each of the instances mentioned above, those who made the rulings to kill the babies were inconvenienced in some way because of a baby. Likewise, those who kill babies today through abortion do so because they feel their life is being inconvenienced. The person who wants the child killed should have thought about their decision to have pleasure with someone before they enjoyed the pleasures of marriage. Just because your life is going to be inconvenienced doesn't make murder right.

8. God will punish those who shed innocent blood.

Joel 3:19 says, *"Egypt shall be a desolation, and Edom shall be a desolate wilderness, for* the violence against the children of Judah, because they have shed innocent blood in their land." Notice that God promised to desolate Egypt and Edom because they shed innocent blood. You cannot kill the innocent blood of babies in the womb of their mother and expect God to stand by idly. God will punish every nation, person, and doctor who chooses to kill babies in the womb.

9. Abortion is not right just because a child may be deemed abnormal.

Isaiah 49:16 says, "Behold, I have graven thee upon the palms of my hands; thy walls are continually before me." Many doctors have talked parents into murdering their child in the mother's womb because they said the child was going to be "abnormal." May I ask you, who are these doctors to think that they know what is normal or abnormal? God says that He carved the hands of a little infant. What some may consider "abnormal" is God's creation, and nobody has a right to take that life just because they don't like how God may have made that child.

When my wife was with child, they told us that our daughter was going to be abnormal. The doctor tried to urge my wife to "abort" (murder) the baby. Of course, we did not do that, and that baby that was born is now my church pianist. Just because a baby may be "deemed not normal" does not give you a right to kill that baby in its mother's womb.

10. God is the only One who is to take life.

Hebrews 9:27 says, *"And as it is appointed unto men once to die, but after this the judgment:"* God is the only One who is to appoint the day of one's death, not a doctor. Job 1:21 reiterated this when Job said, *"...the LORD gave, and the LORD hath taken away; blessed be the name of the LORD."* My friend, you are not to play God in anyone's life. That life inside of the womb of a lady is a creation of God. Only God has the right to take life, not man.

When you consider all of these verses, it is not hard to conclude that life begins at conception, and to take that life is murder. It may not be convenient to keep that life for whatever reason, but it is always right to allow that life to be born.

CHAPTER THREE

ALCOHOL

Proverbs 23:29-30 says, *"Who hath woe? who hath sorrow? who hath contentions? who hath babbling? who hath wounds without cause? who hath redness of eyes? They that tarry long at the wine; they that go to seek mixed wine."* The Scriptures are very clear about the sin of alcohol. Sadly, many never look at the dangers of alcohol, and to their own detriment. It is said that nearly 86% of adults have drank alcohol at some point in their life.

The dangers of alcohol cannot be overstated. It is said that alcohol is a factor in 40% of all violent crimes. I was talking to a police officer in Anchorage, Alaska, several years ago, and he told me that alcohol was involved in nearly 70% of all the crimes in his city. In other words, crime would drastically drop if alcohol were not a part of our society.

The influence of alcohol and sin is obvious. Alcohol is the cause of many young people losing their purity. When it comes to alcohol in general (aside from the Scriptures), it is bad for your health, family, and career to drink alcohol. Even if the Scriptures were not clear on alcohol, its effect on society and families alone should be the greatest warning against drinking it. However, the Scriptures are very clear about the dangers of alcohol, and whether or not it is a sin to drink it.

Alcohol is defined as either *"wine"* or *"strong drink"* in the Scriptures. When the Scriptures use the word *"wine,"* we must look at the context to see if it is talking about grape juice or alcohol. For instance, we know that Jesus would never contribute to sin; therefore, when He turned the water into wine, He was turning the water into grape juice. The reason the people noticed the difference was because it wasn't watered down. Jesus turned the water into pure grape juice, which is what got the attention of those in the wedding party. Let me show you what the Scriptures teach about alcohol, and why it is a sin.

1. Alcohol makes a mockery of your life.

Proverbs 20:1 says, *"Wine is a mocker, strong drink is raging: and whosoever is deceived thereby is not wise."* People do foolish things when under the influence of alcohol. Crimes, immorality, and anger are common when someone is under the influence of alcohol. If you don't want your life to be a laughingstock, you would be wise to stay away from alcohol.

2. Alcohol often leads to immorality.

In Genesis 9:21-23, Noah got drunk which led to his son committing immorality with him.

In Genesis 19:31-36, alcohol is what caused Lot to be immoral with his daughters, which led to them being with child. These men would have never committed immorality had they not been drunk.

Many young people lose their purity on the night of their prom because of alcohol. Many adults have committed adultery while they were under the influence of alcohol. Alcohol is the enemy of purity. If you want to live a moral life, you would be wise to stay away from alcohol.

3. Alcohol hurts innocent people.

Proverbs 20:1 says, *"...strong drink is raging..."* Many people have reacted in a rage because they were under the influence of alcohol. Prisons are filled with men who beat their wives while under the influence of alcohol. Many murders have been committed because someone got angry while they were drunk. If you don't want to hurt those you love, you would be wise to stay away from alcohol.

4. Drinking alcohol is not wise.

Proverbs 20:1 continues to say, *"...whosoever is deceived thereby is not wise."* It is wise not to drink alcohol, because you might do something you would regret while you are under its influence. Wise people know how alcohol hurts their health, family, and careers, and they will stay away from it because they don't want it to destroy their future.

5. Alcohol is addicting.

Proverbs 23:35 says, *"They have stricken me, shalt thou say, and I was not sick; they have beaten me, and I felt it not: when shall I awake? I will seek it yet again."* It's a sad statement when someone has been hurt by alcohol, but they will *"seek it yet again."* Why would someone seek the very thing that has hurt them? They will seek it because they are addicted to it. You must understand that you are capable of being addicted to any sin because you are a sinner. Alcohol's pull is greater than many imagine. It lies to you and tells you that you can control it; yet, you still run back to it because you are addicted. The only one who is to control you is the Holy Ghost and not alcohol.

6. Alcohol causes you not to be filled with the Holy Spirit.

Ephesians 5:18 says, *"And be not drunk with wine, wherein is excess; but be filled with the Spirit;"* If there is any reason that reveals that alcohol is a sin, it is that you can't be controlled by alcohol and the Holy Ghost at the same time. Interestingly, that God compares the filling of the Holy Spirit to alcohol. The reason He uses this comparison is because people will do things they normally would not do when under the influence of alcohol; likewise, believers will do things they normally would not do when filled with the Holy Spirit. It is a sin not to be filled and controlled by the Holy Spirit; therefore, drinking alcohol is a sin.

7. Alcohol consumption of any amount is sin.

Casual drinking is like casual sin; it is still a sin. Social drinking is like social sin; all sin is wrong. Romans 6:23 says, *"For the wages of sin is death..."* God didn't say casual or social sin, but He said sin. Proverbs 20:1 says, *"Wine is a mocker, strong drink is raging..."* God didn't say how much you had to drink for wine to be a mocker; He just said that it *"is a mocker."* The very first sip of alcohol is a sin and makes a mockery of you. Just because you drink alcohol casually or at social events doesn't change its effects. Alcohol is wrong at any level of consumption.

8. Alcohol is a work of the flesh.

Galatians 5:19 says, *"Now the works of the flesh are manifest, which are these;..."* In verse 21, God says that *"drunkenness"* is one of the works of the flesh. A person cannot get drunk without first drinking alcohol. Galatians 5:17 says, *"For the flesh lusteth against the Spirit, and the Spirit against the flesh: and these are contrary the one to the other: so that ye cannot do the things that ye would."* You cannot serve God and fulfill the desires of alcohol at the same time. It's impossible to please God and drink alcohol at the same time.

9. Alcohol clouds your judgment.

Isaiah 28:7 says, *"But they also have erred through wine, and through strong drink are out of the way; the priest and the prophet have erred through strong drink, they are swallowed up of wine, they are out of the way through*

27

strong drink; they err in vision, they stumble in judgment." Notice how alcohol caused these people to err and to get out of the right way of living. You will never serve God successfully and drink alcohol at the same time. Your ability to make the right decisions while under the influence of alcohol is impaired. One reason it is illegal to drink alcohol and drive is because it impairs your ability to make quick decisions. You are one decision away from making a tragic decision, and you won't know when the decision is going to have to be made; therefore, if you don't want your judgment clouded, you should never drink alcohol.

10. Alcohol causes you to say things you will later regret.

The Scriptures say when talking about alcohol in Proverbs 23:33, *"...thine heart shall utter perverse things."* Many people have said foolish things that they later regretted while they were drunk. Your ability to control your mouth while you are under alcohol's influence is impaired, and likely you will say things that will hurt your relationships and the ones who you love.

11. Alcohol leads to a life of regret and heartache.

God shows the conclusion of alcohol on one's life in Proverbs 23:32 when He says, *"At the last it biteth like a serpent, and stingeth like an adder."* Many people have lived the rest of their life regretting what they did while under alcohol's influence. If you don't want to experience the heartache and regret that alcohol causes, you would be wise to avoid having one drink of alcohol. Alcohol is still the Devil's beverage, and anyone who consumes it will only find heartache at the end.

CHAPTER FOUR

DANCING

Dancing is one of those activities that are often not discussed because of the confusion Satan tries to create. There are two types of dancing in the Scriptures. The first type of dancing described in the Scriptures is nothing more than excitement and rejoicing. 1 Samuel 18:6 shows dancing as rejoicing when it says, *"And it came to pass as they came, when David was returned from the slaughter of the Philistine, that the women came out of all cities of Israel, singing and dancing, to meet king Saul, with tabrets, with joy, and with instruments of musick."* These people were excited that they had just won a battle, and they sang and danced, which is nothing more than a rejoicing moment as they praised God. David did the same thing when he brought up the ark of God. It says in 2 Samuel 6:14, *"And David danced before the LORD with all his might; and David was girded with a linen ephod.*" In both of these instances, dancing was a mere result of rejoicing. This type of dancing is nothing more than what we do when we jump up and down in excitement as we cheer for our sports team.

There is another type of dancing mentioned in the Scriptures, and this is the type of dancing that is wrong. In Exodus 32:19, it says that Moses saw Israel *"dancing"* around a golden calf. The music that was being played was not of a spiritual nature, because the music being played sounded more like a war than it did like God's music.

Galatians 5:16 says, *"This I say then, Walk in the Spirit, and ye shall not fulfil the lust of the flesh."* The dancing of today is more like the second type of dancing that is lust-filled, and fleshly driven. There is little question that the Scriptures are against this fleshy-driven, lust-filled dancing that appeals to the flesh. This

31

modern-day dancing that is done to appease the flesh is wrong for several reasons.

1. Dancing is wrong because it often accentuates intimate motions.

Ephesians 5:3 says, *"But fornication, and all uncleanness, or covetousness, let it not be once named among you, as becometh saints;"* The modern dancing that mimics intimacy between two people is merely making fornication seem acceptable. Fornication is a sin, and dancing that would accentuate it is a sin. 1 Thessalonians 5:22 says, *"Abstain from all appearance of evil."* Dancing that is done to look like fornication and adultery is a sin.

2. Dancing is wrong because a man should not touch a woman.

1 Corinthians 7:1 says, *"Now concerning the things whereof ye wrote unto me: It is good for a man not to touch a woman."* This

verse is talking about touching someone to whom you are not married. If it is good not to touch a woman to whom you are not married, that means it is bad to touch them. When two people are dancing together, they must touch each other; therefore, it is clear that dancing is a sin.

3. Dancing is wrong because it arouses lust in the mind.

People dance to draw attention to other parts of their body other than their face. The purpose is to attract the opposite sex's attention in a way that would cause them to lust. Matthew 5:28 says, *"But I say unto you, That whosoever looketh on a woman to lust after her hath committed adultery with her already in his heart."* A woman dancing is going to promote lust in the mind of a young man. A young woman cannot flaunt her body in a fornicating matter and not bring lust to the mind of a young man.

God commands in 2 Timothy 2:22, *"Flee also youthful lusts..."* Anything that could cause another person to lust after your body is wrong. God commands us to flee any action or activity that would create lusts in the mind.

4. Dancing is wrong because it is often performed with carnal music.

In Exodus 32:18-19, the children of Israel were not dancing to *"Amazing Grace."* They were playing music that sounded like a war, which is nothing more than the rock music of our day. I seriously doubt that anyone can dance in a fleshly manner to spiritual music. The fact that it takes carnal music to dance in itself makes dancing wrong.

5. Dancing is wrong because it is often done in worldly places.

2 Corinthians 6:17 says, *"Wherefore come out from among them, and be ye separate,*

saith the Lord…" God commands the believer to come out of the world. Dancing is not done in spiritual places, but in sin-filled places. Clubs and rock concerts are certainly not a place where the LORD would want you to be; however, these are the places where people go dancing. The places where people must go to dance makes dancing wrong.

6. Dancing is wrong because it tempts you to sin.

James 1:14-15 says, *"But every man is tempted, when he is drawn away of his own lust, and enticed. Then when lust hath conceived, it bringeth forth sin: and sin, when it is finished, bringeth forth death."* Dancing is performed to draw a lustful eye towards your body to cause a lustful mind to think wrong thoughts about it. The next step after lust is sin. God commands the believer in Ephesians 4:27, *"Neither give place to the devil."* You are giving the Devil a chance to ruin your mind

35

through lust when you dance and go to the places where dancing is done.

7. Dancing is wrong because its sole purpose is to please the flesh.

1 John 2:16 says, *"For all that is in the world, the lust of the flesh, and the lust of the eyes, and the pride of life, is not of the Father, but is of the world."* There is no other purpose for dancing other than to please the flesh. Any action that is done to fill your lust is not of God; therefore, it is a sin.

8. Dancing is wrong because it looks wrong.

1 Thessalonians 5:22 commands the believer to *"Abstain from all appearance of evil."* You cannot look at someone who is dancing and say that it looks like a spiritual action. The fact that dancing looks like someone is trying to bring attention to parts of their body that should not be accentuated makes dancing

wrong. If it looks wrong, you are to do everything you can to stay away from it.

9. Dancing is wrong because it is of the world.

1 John 2:15-16 says, *"Love not the world, neither the things that are in the world. If any man love the world, the love of the Father is not in him. For all that is in the world, the lust of the flesh, and the lust of the eyes, and the pride of life, is not of the Father, but is of the world."* God did not originate the type of dancing that mimics fornication, the world did. The fact that dancing is a worldly source of fleshly entertainment makes it a sin.

10. Dancing is wrong because you can't please the flesh and God at the same time.

James 4:4 says, *"Ye adulterers and adulteresses, know ye not that the friendship of the world is enmity with God? whosoever therefore will be a friend of the world is the enemy of God."* Simply put, whatever you do to please the flesh displeases God. You cannot please both at the same time.

My friend, you cannot look at dancing in light of the Scriptures and say there is nothing wrong with it. The purpose of dancing is to please the flesh, feed your lusts, and promote promiscuity; therefore, dancing obviously is a sin against God.

CHAPTER FIVE

GAMBLING

I have preached in Reno, Nevada, many times. Every time I get off the plane and go through the terminal, I see slot machines right there to tempt the passenger to start gambling. When you look at the city at night, you see a city that is lit up, and the casinos having pretty lights that invite you to come in; however, behind those flashing lights are people wasting their money away in an atmosphere that promotes sin.

Gambling has always been a sin, and it is still a sin. Just because the government legalizes gambling that doesn't make it right. They can try to package gambling in a casino, lottery, poker tables, horse and dog racing, or even in sports, but it is still a sin no matter how it is done. These institutions of sin promise to make you a lot of money, but that is nothing more than a facade that covers broken homes, an increase of crime, and sin-broken lives. The Scriptures show several reasons why gambling is a sin. Let me share with you just a few of the reasons why gambling is a sin and MUST be avoided.

1. Gambling is wrong because it is addictive.

God says in 1 Corinthians 6:12, "*All things are lawful unto me, but all things are not expedient: all things are lawful for me, but I will not be brought under the power of any.*" Nothing is to control a believer other than the Holy Spirit of God. Gambling has a way of causing people to go back to it just like the drug addict runs back to drugs. Gambling's pull is that you can win it all and never have to work again, which at its best is against the Scriptures. The gambling institutions make a play on your flesh hoping that you will try it one time because they know that nobody ever stops gambling after the first try.

2. Gambling is wrong because it is a result of a love for money.

1 Timothy 6:10 says, *"For the love of money is the root of all evil: which while some coveted after, they have erred from the faith, and pierced themselves through with many sorrows."* Money in itself is not evil, but it is the love of money that becomes evil. The evil's of gambling are the families that go without because someone's love for money causes them to run back to the gambling institution in hopes of winning more money.

3. Gambling is wrong because it is a result of greed.

Proverbs 15:27 says, *"He that is greedy of gain troubleth his own house; but he that hateth gifts shall live."* Greed drives the gambler. Once they win, they have to keep going because they believe that they can win more. Gambling baits the individual with a little winning to get them to keep spending until they leave broke. It is greed that keeps a person from walking away from gambling.

4. Gambling is wrong because it is a result of covetousness.

Why would a person gamble? They gamble because they are not content with what they have. Luke 12:15 says, *"And he said unto them, Take heed, and beware of covetousness: for a man's life consisteth not in the abundance of the things which he possesseth."* God commands the believer in Hebrews 13:5, *"Let your conversation be without covetousness; and be content with such things as ye have…"* The person controlled by gambling is merely responding to their covetous appetite that wants more than what God has already given them.

5. Gambling is wrong because it leads to other sins.

James 4:7 says, *"Submit yourselves therefore to God. Resist the devil, and he will flee from you."* You can only overcome sin by resisting the places where sin is advertised and committed. You will always find that alcohol, prostitution, and drugs are commonplace at establishments of gambling. Satan knows that if he can get a person addicted to gambling that he can probably get them addicted to other sins. You never just gamble without eventually getting involved in other sins.

6. Gambling is wrong because you should work for what you get.

God established his principle for making money in Genesis 3:19 when He says, *"In the sweat of thy face shalt thou eat bread..."* People are to earn money by working, and not through chance. Furthermore, 2 Thessalonians

3:10 says, *"…if any would not work, neither should he eat."* Gambling subverts God's command to work for money.

7. Gambling is wrong because it always leads to wanting more.

Ecclesiastes 5:10 says, *"He that loveth silver shall not be satisfied with silver; nor he that loveth abundance with increase: this is also vanity."* Gambling never satisfies the soul. If you did win "big" in gambling, you would still not be satisfied because gambling leaves you empty and unfulfilled. You cannot do wrong and find satisfaction and fulfillment in doing it.

8. Gambling is wrong because you cannot serve God and gamble simultaneously.

Luke 16:13 says, *"No servant can serve two masters: for either he will hate the one, and love the other; or else he will hold to the one, and despise the other. Ye cannot serve God* and mammon." It is impossible to be right with God and gamble at the same time. You can't feed covetousness and be right with God. You can't be in places of sin and expect to find God's favor. If you choose to gamble, it will become your master; therefore, you cannot be in love with God when you are serving the master of gambling.

9. Gambling is wrong because it robs money from responsibilities.

Proverbs 28:22 says, "He that hasteth to be rich hath an evil eye, and considereth not that poverty shall come upon him." Gambling is evil because it will take food out of a child's mouth so that a parent can feed their gambling addiction. Gambling is evil because it takes money away from the financial responsibilities that you are to pay every month. The pathway of gambling always leads to poverty. The casino always wins, and the gambler always loses.

10. Gambling is wrong because it is putting your trust in chance instead of the LORD.

1 Timothy 6:17 says, *"Charge them that are rich in this world, that they be not highminded, nor trust in uncertain riches, but in the living God, who giveth us richly all things to enjoy;"* God's command to the believer is to trust Him and not money. The gambler's hope is that they will win big so that they never have to worry about money again. Philippians 4:19 says, *"But my God shall supply all your need according to his riches in glory by Christ Jesus."* Gambling is trusting chance to supply your needs instead of God, which is nothing more than idolatry.

My friend, never allow yourself to get involved with this sin. It will control you and leave you financially broke. Instead of gambling and leaving your financial future to chance, trust God to supply your needs and work hard. Remember that most, if not all, wealthy people have acquired their wealth through hard work and not through gambling.

CHAPTER SIX

DATING AS A CHRISTIAN

The importance of friends can never be overemphasized, but the importance of who you marry absolutely influences the rest of your life. People go to college for four years, and sometimes more, to prepare for a career, but most people start dating and get married without any preparation. It is no wonder that so many people end up divorced, and so many young people lose their purity when we consider how irresponsible we are about young people dating.

Let me make it clear that I don't really care whether you call it dating or courting because neither word is scriptural. If you really wanted to use scriptural terminology, you would call it finding a wife. Proverbs 18:22 says, *"Whoso findeth a wife findeth a good thing, and obtaineth favour of the LORD."* For the sake of what I have called it for years, I will talk about dating.

God does make it clear that the man is to find a wife, not the woman find a husband. I am not saying that a girl shouldn't be friendly to a guy, but she shouldn't be flirty with boys because she will attract the wrong type of young man. There are several principles that young people need to follow when it comes to dating so that they can find the right spouse and stay pure while they are dating. Let me share these principles with you.

1. Have spiritual relationships.

You can't like the wrong person if you don't have the wrong friends. The best way to keep yourself from dating the wrong person is to make sure all of your friendships are spiritual friendships. Proverbs 2:20 says, *"That thou mayest walk in the way of good men, and keep the paths of the righteous."* You will find the right type of person to date while you are walking in the *"paths of the righteous."* Always remember that whoever you date should be someone with whom you were first friends. Therefore, keeping spiritual relationships and friendships is critical to dating and marrying the right person.

2. Keep a close relationship with your parents.

Ephesians 6:2 says, *"Honour thy father and mother..."* The best thing any young person can do to help them find the right person to date is to keep a good relationship with their parents. Your relationship with your parents will pass over to whomever you marry. If you don't have a good relationship with your parents, you will find that you will struggle in your marriage. You must find a way not only to get along with your parents, but you must also build your relationship with them so that you know how to have a right relationship with others.

3.   Never date someone who is not saved.

2 Corinthians 6:14 says, *"Be ye not unequally yoked together with unbelievers..."* I know that everyone has heard this many times, but many people don't heed this warning and God's command. If you don't want to marry someone who is lost, you had better not date someone who is lost. You can't "fall in love" with a lost person if you are not dating them. It is a sin to yoke up in a dating relationship with a lost person just as much as it is wrong to marry a lost person.

4.   Never date someone just to date.

You should always have a purpose for dating a person. One reason people get themselves into trouble is because they feel like they have to date someone because of the world's pressure on them; therefore, they lower their standards of who to date just so that they can date. It is always better not to date at all than it is to date someone just to have a date. It was when Dinah went out to see the daughters of the land in Genesis 34, that she met the wrong young man and ended up losing her purity. Always have a purpose for dating a person, and that purpose should be to find the person with whom you can serve the LORD for the rest of your lives.

5. Never date someone who you would not want your children to be like.

Proverbs 27:17 says, *"Iron sharpeneth iron; so a man sharpeneth the countenance of his friend."* Your children will become like whomever you marry; therefore, you must be careful who you date because you will marry a person that you date. Always ask yourself before dating an individual if you would want your children to be like them. If you wouldn't want your children to turn out like that person, you must then choose not to date them.

6. Never date someone who is not serving the LORD.

2 Corinthians 6:14, applies to this principle. Amos 3:3 also asks, *"Can two walk together, except they be agreed?"* The best way to find someone to marry is by staying busy serving the LORD. You will find that those you serve the LORD with will become the best people to date. If a person is not serving the LORD, you should never date them. The philosophy that you will make them a better person doesn't work. A weaker person always pulls the stronger person down; therefore, don't date someone who is spiritually weak.

7. Never date someone who has recently changed to get your attention.

Proverbs 24:21 says, *"... meddle not with them that are given to change:"* Just because someone has recently started serving the LORD doesn't mean you should date them;

53

instead, you would be wise to wait several months to see if they are going to stick to their decision to serve the LORD.

8. Love is stupid — give someone veto power.

Proverbs 11:14 says, *"Where no counsel is, the people fall: but in the multitude of counsellors there is safety."* People often say that love is blind, but I often say it is stupid. People do stupid things because they are "in love." You will not see things that others can see when you think you are in love with someone. The greatest safeguard you can have is to give someone veto-power in your dating life, and listen to them when they tell you to break it off. I believe your parents should have veto-power in your life, and I also believe you would be wise to give your pastor or his wife the same power. These are people who love you and want the best for you, and they will see things in your life that you can't

54

see. You would be wise to listen to them when they tell you someone is not the right person for you.

9. Plan your time together.

In Proverbs 7, a young man was just passing through the streets when the wrong lady lured him in and caused him to be immoral. Likewise, many young people lose their purity because they don't plan their time together. When you choose to go on a date, plan what you are going to do, and when you are done, be done.

10. NEVER be alone.

1 Corinthians 6:18 says, *"Flee fornication."* 2 Timothy 2:22 also says, *"Flee also youthful lusts..."* You can't be alone with the opposite sex and not open yourself to the temptation of immorality. The best way to flee immorality is to never be alone with a person of the

opposite sex. You can't be immoral with someone you are dating if you always have an adult chaperone with you.

11. Never touch.

1 Corinthians 7:1 says, *"Now concerning the things whereof ye wrote unto me: It is good for a man not to touch a woman."* This verse is talking to single people. If God is saying it is good not to touch a woman, He is then saying that it is bad to touch a woman. If you never touch the opposite sex before marriage, you will never have to worry about losing your purity.

12. Never hide your relationship with someone.

Hiding your relationship with someone is deceptive, and deception is the root of all relationship problems. God says in Proverbs 27:5, *"Open rebuke is better than secret love."* The fact that you are hiding your relationship proves that you are being deceptive. If it is right, you won't have to hide it. You should always get your parent's approval before you start dating someone.

13. Ask God to send you the right person to marry.

Matthew 7:7 says, *"Ask, and it shall be given you; seek, and ye shall find; knock, and it shall be opened unto you:"* James 4:2 says, *"...ye have not, because ye ask not."* Now is an excellent time to start asking God to help you find the right spouse. God wants you to find the right person more than you do, so ask Him to help you find that person.

14. Listen to your gut.

There are times when you have a little voice in your gut that tells you something is wrong. Let me encourage you to listen to that voice because that voice is probably the voice of the Holy Spirit. That little voice is probably the *"still small voice"* of 1 Kings 19:12. Don't lower your standards just because you like someone. Listen to the voice of the Holy Spirit when He tries to warn you about a person. It is always better to break off a relationship than it is to go forward and ignore the voice to your own detriment.

Dating is vital to your walk with Christ. If you plan on serving the LORD for the rest of your life, you had better be sure to date the right people. Whomever you marry will influence what you do with your life, so be sure to date the right type of people so you can stay pure and not marry the wrong kind of person.

CHAPTER SEVEN

WHY CHURCH IS IMPORTANT

How often one is commanded to go to church is one of the tools backslidden believers often use to excuse their lack of church attendance. Of course, Satan is thrilled when people don't go to church because he knows it will keep them from becoming what they are supposed to be.

As a child growing up, my parents never gave me a choice about going to church. They rightfully required me to go to church every time the church doors were open. One of the great Baptist pastors from the past, Dr. Lee Roberson, used to always say that it takes three to thrive. He meant that a believer never grows as they should unless they attend church both services on Sunday, and also attend the Wednesday night Bible study and prayer time. My parents took his advice and followed the teachings of Scriptures, and taught me the importance of going to church three times a week.

Sadly, many say that the Scriptures teach that we are only required to go to church once a week. That may sound good to a person who doesn't have a heart to serve the LORD, but it is in direct contradiction to the command and examples found in the Scriptures. Let me share with you several scriptural reasons as to why church is important and why attending it is critical to your Christian growth.

1. Church is commanded.

Hebrews 10:25 says, *"Not forsaking the assembling of ourselves together, as the manner of some is; but exhorting one another: and so much the more, as ye see the day approaching."* The word *"assembling"* is the same word for church. In other words, God is saying, *"Not forsaking the churching of* ourselves together." You will notice that this is not a choice, but a command. God commands the believer to gather with the church whenever it gathers for a service. Missing one service a week is being disobedient to God's Word. It doesn't matter if you think that service is not important because God commands you to attend. Likewise, when the church assembles for special meetings, you are to attend those services as well.

2. Night church is scriptural.

Acts 20:7-8 says, *"And upon the first day of the week, when the disciples came together to break bread, Paul preached unto them, ready to depart on the morrow; and continued his speech until midnight. And there were many lights in the upper chamber, where they were gathered together."* There are a couple of things I want you to see about these verses. The first thing is that they met on the *"first day of the week."* The second thing I want you to

61

see is that the services went until midnight and there were *"many lights"* in the place where they met. We have Sunday night services because we are copying the example of the church in Acts that had Sunday night services.

Moreover, in Acts 12:12-18, you have the story of Peter being delivered from jail. The first place he went after he was delivered was to the church house. It was some time in the middle of the week, and the church was having a prayer meeting. The reason we have midweek services is because of the example of the church of Jerusalem having a midweek prayer meeting. This is one of the reasons that churches call their midweek service a prayer meeting. The day that the church meets is not as important as to it meeting in the middle of the week. Whether a church has a midweek service on Tuesday, Wednesday, or Thursday is not important, but what is important is that a church follows the example of the church in Acts 12 that had a midweek service.

3. You should be faithful to church because it's important to God.

Ephesians 5:25 says, *"Husbands, love your wives, even as Christ also loved the church, and gave himself for it;"* If Jesus was willing to die for the church, the least you could do is be faithful to all the services of the church. Church is important, and you should be faithful to it because of the sacrificial price that Christ made for it.

4. You should be faithful to church because God commands you to be faithful.

Hebrews 10:25 says, *"Not forsaking the assembling of ourselves together, as the manner of some is..."* *"Not forsaking"* is the same as the command to be faithful. In other words, God is telling the believer to "be faithful to the assembling of ourselves together." The command to be faithful to church is not the preacher's command or desire, but it is God's command. How many services is the believer to be faithful to? The believer is to be faithful to as many services as the church assembles together.

5. You should be faithful to church because it is where you receive encouragement.

The reason the believer is not to forsake the assembling of the believers is so that they can be an encouragement to each other. Hebrews 10:25 continues to say, *"Not forsaking the assembling of ourselves together, as the manner of some is; but exhorting one another..."* You will find that you will get the encouragement you need when you go to church; encouragement from the preaching as well as encouragement from fellow believers. Moreover, you need to be faithful to church because your church attendance encourages others to attend. You always drag another believer out of church when you become unfaithful to church. Your faithfulness to every service is important for you to receive encouragement as well as your being an encouragement to others.

6. Being faithful to church allows you to learn God's Word.

Titus 1:3 says, *"But hath in due times manifested his word through preaching, which is committed unto me according to the commandment of God our Saviour;"* The manifesting of God's Word is to dissect it so that people can understand it. God commanded the church in Acts 20:28 to *"feed the church of God."* You can certainly learn from personal study time in God's Word, but you are going to find that God's Word will be explained in a practical manner to you by going to Sunday school and church. It could be that the one service you miss is the one with a truth that can change your life.

7. Being faithful to church keeps you out of the world.

2 Corinthians 6:17 says, *"Wherefore come out from among them..."* The words *"come out"* rightly define the church. A church is a local, "called out" assembly. In other words, coming out to church gets you out of the world. You will more easily overcome the world by being faithful to church.

8. Being faithful to church helps you to fight sin better.

2 Corinthians 6:17 continues to say, *"... come out from among them, and be ye separate, saith the Lord, and touch not the unclean thing..."* The *"unclean thing"* in this verse is sin. You will have a much easier time overcoming sin by being faithful to church than

you will by missing church. By being faithful to church, you will learn how to fight sin better. By coming out of the world, you are leaving the place that promotes sin to going to a place the promotes righteousness and holiness. You will find yourself acquiring a distaste for sin the more faithful you are to church. Those who miss church will struggle in their battle to overcome sin.

9. You should be faithful to church because it helps you to have the right friends.

Paul said in Philemon 1:2, *"And to our beloved Apphia, and Archippus our fellowsoldier, and to the church in thy house:"* Paul met these people in church. Often, in the Pauline epistles, you will read about Paul greeting certain people. These were friends who he met while attending church. You have a better chance of having the right friends by being faithful to church. While you are at church, be friendly with those who attend the services. Getting involved in the church ministries will help you to cultivate friends who have a righteous mindset and who have a heart to please the LORD. The right friends will never be found in the wrong places. Friendships that are discovered through serving God will have the common bond of serving God and doing right which will help you to continue doing right.

10. Church is important because it challenges you to serve the LORD.

Acts 5:11 says, *"And great fear came upon all the church..."* This verse is the result of God killing Ananias and Sapphira. You will notice how the church was challenged to do right by God's action. You will never be challenged to serve the LORD by living in the world, but you find that challenge by going to church. Most people who are unfaithful to church are people who do little to serve the LORD. Church is important because it is where you are challenged to live by faith and to do more for God.

11. Church is important because it gives you a place to bring those whom you've led to Christ.

Acts 2:47 says, *"Praising God, and having favour with all the people. And the Lord added to the church daily such as should be saved."* The only way people can be added to the church is if they are baptized. Church is the place where you bring those whom you've led to Christ to have them added to the church. Being faithful to church challenges you to be a better soul winner and to get your converts to church.

12. Church is important because it is a place you can pray.

Acts 12:5 says, *"Peter therefore was kept in prison: but prayer was made without ceasing of the church unto God for him."* One of the reasons churches have a midweek service is so that the church can pray together for the needs of others. You can certainly pray on your own, but the Scriptures make it clear that it is also good for the church to pray together.

Always remember that the more important church is important to you, the more God will be important to you. Let me encourage you to stay faithful to church so that you can keep your heart warm towards God.

CHAPTER EIGHT

WHY THE KING JAMES BIBLE

God's Word has always been under attack. It was attacked first in the Garden of Eden when Satan asked Eve in Genesis 3:1, "...*Yea, hath God said...?*" Since this time, this has been Satan's tactic concerning God's Word and anything God commands the believer to do. Satan questions God's Word to create doubt in the mind of the believer because he knows that you can only succeed in your Christian walk through faith. Doubt is the enemy of faith, so if Satan can create doubt in your mind about the authenticity of God's Word, he can get you to fail to walk by faith.

The same question that Satan presented to Eve is being used today by liberals who want God's Word to fit their lives instead of their lives fitting God's Word. These liberal preachers who question the King James Bible only do this so that they can become your authority. Whether or not they admit this, they want to be God in your life. These who question whether God is able to preserve His Word in the English language through the King James Bible simply do this so that you have to run to them to find out what is and is not true. Let me share with you several scriptural reasons as to why we use the King James Bible.

1. God's Word was settled in Heaven before there was a preservation on Earth.

God's Word was in Heaven before the Earth was created. Psalm 119:89 says, *"For ever, O LORD, thy word is settled in heaven."* *"For ever"* means that there is no beginning or ending. In other words, God's Word was in Heaven before He created this Earth; therefore, any writing of God's Word, including the Hebrew and Greek, is a preservation of

God's Word that was settled in Heaven. When you understand that even the Hebrew and Greek texts were a preservation of God's Word, you will then realize that God can give us His perfect and inspired Word in the English language.

2. The only originals are in Heaven.

If God's Word was settled in Heaven as Psalm 119:89 says, then the "originals" are only in Heaven. According to John 1:1, Jesus Christ is the original Word of God. This verse says, *"In the beginning was the Word, and the Word was with God, and the Word was God."* God further proves that Jesus Christ is the Word in John 1:14 where it says, *"And the Word was made flesh, and dwelt among us, (and we beheld his glory, the glory as of the only begotten of the Father,) full of grace and truth."* The originals are NOT the Hebrew and Greek text, the originals are in Heaven. The Hebrew and Greek text are only a preservation of the originals that are in Heaven. When you hear the word "originals" as referring to the Hebrew and Greek, you must watch out for that person because they are about to change God's Word on you.

3. It is God's job to preserve His Word.

Psalm 12:6-7 says, *"The words of the LORD are pure words: as silver tried in a furnace of earth, purified seven times. Thou shalt keep them, O LORD, thou shalt preserve them from this generation for ever."* One of the mistakes many people make is to think that it is man's job to preserve His Word. God valued His Word so much that He left the preservation of it to Himself. To doubt that God could preserve His Word in the King James Bible is to doubt the power of God to be able to preserve His Word. Just like God doesn't need your help to get saved or to keep your salvation, He also does not need man's help to keep His Word preserved for every generation.

4. God used men to preserve His Word.

2 Peter 1:21 says, *"For the prophecy came not in old time by the will of man: but holy men of God spake as they were moved by the Holy Ghost."* Many people use this verse errantly to refer that this verse is talking about inspiration of the Scriptures. This verse is not at all talking about inspiration, but this verse is referring to preservation of the Scriptures. God, in His power, used sinful men to preserve His Word. As the psalmist says in Psalm 45:1, *"… my tongue is the pen of a ready writer."* God literally controlled the men as a person would control a writing object to preserve His Word for this generation. The men were not inspired, but God's Word is what is inspired. The men were simply a pen in the hand of God to write what He wanted them to write. God didn't fit His Word to each writer's personality, but He created each person whom He would use to preserve His Word with their personality.

5. Every word of God must be preserved to be His Word.

Matthew 5:18 says, *"For verily I say unto you, Till heaven and earth pass, one jot or one tittle shall in no wise pass from the law, till all be fulfilled."* God said that the littlest part of His Word must be preserved to be His Word. God says in Proverbs 30:5, *"Every word of God is pure"* He didn't say most of the words were inspired, but *"every word"* of God is pure and preserved. If there is one word that is not in the King James Bible that God wanted in it, then God failed to keep His Word by giving us an every word Bible.

6. God inspired His words and not a language.

2 Timothy 3:16 says, *"All scripture is given by inspiration of God..."* Here is where most people get messed up. Many people think that God inspired the language of Hebrew and

Greek when God actually inspired His words in Heaven. Therefore, when God preserved His Word in the English language through the King James Bible, He preserved the inspiration of His Word as well. To say that only the originals are inspired is to say that God didn't have the power to preserve the inspiration with it. Let me make this clear, the King James Bible is the inspired and preserved Word of God.

7. If one word is added or missing, it is NOT God's Word.

Revelation 22:18-19 says, *"For I testify unto every man that heareth the words of the prophecy of this book, If any man shall add unto these things, God shall add unto him the plagues that are written in this book: And if any man shall take away from the words of the book of this prophecy, God shall take away his part out of the book of life, and out of the holy city, and from the things which are written in this book."* God was so adamant about every word being preserved that He pronounced a curse on anyone who took away or added to His Word. If a perversion (translation) that you are using is missing one word, it is NOT God's Word and therefore must not be used.

8. **The King James Bible is not "the most accurate translation," but it is the ABSOLUTELY accurate, inspired and preserved Word of God.**

2 Timothy 3:16-17 says, *"**All scripture** is given by inspiration of God..."* Many people like to say that the King James Bible is the most accurate translation, but to make this statement is to say that part of it is not accurate. For instance, if I ate most of the pie, that means there is a part of the pie I did not eat. If I say that I did most of the work, it means that there is a part of the job I did not do. To say that the King James Bible is the most accurate translation means that a person

believes that part if it is not accurate. The King James Bible is NOT the most accurate translation, but it is the ABSOLUTELY accurate, inspired and preserved Word of God.

9. You cannot be who and what God wants you to be without every word of the Scriptures.

2 Timothy 3:16-17 says that the purpose of all Scripture being inspired is so that the *"man of God may be perfect, throughly furnished unto all good works."* No believer will ever be what God wants them to be if they don't have an every word Bible. All of the Scriptures are needed if you are to become who and what God wants you to be.

10. Faith has proven that the King James Bible is God's Word.

Hebrews 11:6 says, *"But without faith it is impossible to please him: for he that cometh*

79

to God must believe that he is, and that he is a rewarder of them that diligently seek him." At the end of the day, it takes faith to believe that God is capable of giving us an inspired and preserved, every word Bible in the King James Bible. My friend, you may not completely understand everything, but you must trust God by faith that He has preserved His Word in the King James Bible.

CHAPTER NINE

MIXED SWIMMING

Summertime comes, and it is not difficult to want to go swimming. The problem with going swimming is that often you swim with the opposite sex. The problem with swimming with the opposite sex is that it is hard to be decent and swim at the same time. The other problem presented with the desire to go swimming is that most people don't have a swimming pool in their backyard, so the public swimming pool is the only place where most people go swimming. Again, you are not going to go swimming in a public pool without having to swim with the opposite sex.

Therein creates a predicament, and that is you can't be indecent without having the wrong thoughts. Moreover, you can't have the wrong thoughts without eventually living out those thoughts in life. God says in Romans

13:14, *"But put ye on the Lord Jesus Christ, and make not provision for the flesh, to fulfil the lusts thereof."* You will never fulfill a lust if you don't make provision for it.

Some might ask, what is mixed swimming? Mixed swimming is simply going swimming with the opposite sex. Let me share several thoughts from the Scriptures about this topic.

1. There is nothing wrong with swimming.

In and of itself, there is nothing wrong with going swimming. In fact, you will find that people swam in the Scriptures. You might recall that Paul and the prisoners swam to land when their ship crashed. These prisoners would have never been able to swim had they not learned to swim earlier in life. Therefore, you must understand that God is not saying that it is a sin to swim. In fact, I believe it is good for young people to learn how to swim so that they will know how if needed.

2. There is nothing wrong with men and women swimming.

Let me make it clear that it is not wrong for men or women to swim. The Scriptures never say that you should not swim if you are a man or a woman. Please understand that I am not saying that it is wrong for either sex to go swimming.

3. It is wrong for men and women to swim together.

As God always gives us something to enjoy, Satan always takes that enjoyment and perverts it. There is nothing wrong of a husband and wife swimming together, but there is something wrong with a man and woman who are not married to swim together. Likewise, it is also wrong for families to swim together when they are dressed indecently. It is just as wrong for you to swim with your family when they are indecent as it is for you to swim with someone you don't know who is the opposite sex.

4. It is wrong to do anything that would create evil in your mind.

Romans 16:19 says, *"...I would have you wise unto that which is good, and simple concerning evil."* God is not against you knowing good, but He is against you knowing evil. Looking at the opposite sex who is dressed indecently will always cause you to have thoughts that are wrong; thus, it is wrong to create this evil in your mind.

5. You can't go mixed swimming without seeing the nakedness of others.

Especially in today's world, you are not going to swim with someone without seeing their nakedness. Leviticus 18:17 describes what nakedness is when it says, *"Thou shalt not uncover the nakedness of a woman and* her daughter, neither shalt thou take her son's daughter, or her daughter's daughter, to uncover her nakedness; for they are her near kinswomen: it is wickedness." 1 Timothy 2:9 says, "In like manner also, that women adorn themselves in modest apparel..." Seeing someone's nakedness is not being modest; therefore, it is wrong to see anyone who is dressed immodestly.

6. God commands us not to look at the nakedness of the opposite sex.

Habakkuk 2:15 says, "Woe unto him that giveth his neighbour drink, that puttest thy bottle to him, and makest him drunken also, THAT THOU MAYEST LOOK ON THEIR NAKEDNESS!" Notice that God does not want you to show your nakedness to another person. Later in this book we will describe what the Scriptures describe as the nakedness of others, but for the sake of brevity let us suffice to say that seeing someone dressed in an indecent manner is a sin.

7. You can't see nakedness and not create lust.

Maybe the best way to prove that seeing someone indecent creates lust in the heart of man is in the story of David and Bathsheba. 2 Samuel 11:2 says, *"And it came to pass in an eveningtide, that David arose from off his bed, and walked upon the roof of the king's house: and from the roof he saw a woman washing herself; and the woman was very beautiful to look upon."* David would have never committed adultery with Bathsheba had he not seen her in an indecent manner. God says in Proverbs 6:25, *"Lust not after her beauty in thine heart; neither let her take thee with her eyelids."* God is trying to keep you from sin; therefore, He commands you not to look at a person who is indecent. My friend, you can't see a person of the opposite sex dressed indecently while they are swimming without having the wrong thoughts.

8. Lust leads to a sin in the heart.

Whether or not anyone wants to admit it, when you see someone dressed indecently at a swimming pool, it is nearly impossible not to lust after them in your heart. Matthew 5:28 says, *"But I say unto you, That whosoever looketh on a woman to lust after her hath committed adultery with her already in his heart."* It is just as wrong to have impure thoughts about someone in your heart as it is to actually commit the sin.

9. Lust leads to immorality.

James 1:14-15 says, *"But every man is tempted, when he is drawn away of his own lust, and enticed. Then when lust hath conceived, it bringeth forth sin: and sin, when it is finished, bringeth forth death."* You will notice that lust *"bringeth forth sin."* In other words, whatever you think about in your heart eventually becomes the actions you commit.

10. Mixed swimming with indecent clothing is wrong.

Leviticus 18:6 says, *"None of you shall approach to any that is near of kin to him, to uncover their nakedness: I am the LORD."* Anything worn in public that would show your nakedness is a sin.

11. Mixed swimming is wrong because it destroys a pure mind.

Philippians 4:8 says, *"Finally, brethren, whatsoever things are true, whatsoever things are honest, whatsoever things are just, WHATSOEVER THINGS ARE PURE, whatsoever things are lovely, whatsoever things are of good report; if there be any virtue, and if there be any praise, think on these things."* My friend, how can you see a person dressed indecently and keep a pure mind at the same time? You can't! Anything that would keep you from having a pure mind must be avoided.

12. Only those who enjoy sin would say that mixed swimming doesn't create unholy thoughts.

Titus 1:15 says, *"Unto the pure all things are pure: but unto them that are defiled and unbelieving is nothing pure; but even their mind and conscience is defiled."* Only a scorner who wants to continue to feed their lust will say that looking at someone indecent in the swimming pool doesn't cause them to lust. God created men to desire the woman; therefore, creating unholy thoughts by looking at someone dressed indecently is sin.

CHAPTER TEN

MUSIC

When I was a teenage boy, there was about a 6-month period when I listened to rock music. Though I was not considered a rebellious teenager at the time, the influence it had on my walk with Christ was very evident to me. My desire to read the Scriptures grew cold. I grew a distaste for spiritual music, and my interest to the preaching of God's Word diminished.

It was in a chapel service at school that turned everything around. The principal at our school preached a sermon on rock music, and he said that he would kick out any student who they knew was listening to it. The Holy Spirit's conviction was great on my heart as I knew it was wrong. He asked those who listened to rock music to stay behind after chapel. Though he did not know I was listening to it, I stayed behind because I didn't want to get kicked out of school. As I stayed behind, my mother looked at me in shock. The look of disappointment and shock on her face is what the LORD used to get me to stop listening to it. As soon as I stopped listening to it, my heart for God warmed, my interest in the Scriptures came back, and my love for preaching and soul winning became fervent.

Music is a very controversial topic in Christianity that is often misrepresented in its teaching. The cause of the controversy is because the basis of good music is often based on influences. Four things influence the taste and basis as to whether music is spiritual or carnal.

The first thing that influences the taste of music is preference. Everyone's preference for music is often different. The second influence is the region of the country in which one lives. If a person lived in Kentucky, they may like a bluegrass style of music; whereas, a person in the northeast may totally dislike the bluegrass sound. The region of the country in which you were or are raised does influence your preference. The third influence is the nation in which you live. Every nation has a different sound of music. The music in Mexico is different from the music in the Middle East. The music in the Middle East is very different from the music in the United States. Your music is often influenced by the nation in which you live. The fourth influence is culture. The culture in which you live often dictates the preference in music more than anything else.

At the end of the day, it really doesn't matter what any of these influences say about music; we must ask ourselves if the Scriptures are in agreement with music. Let me point out several things about music to help you to determine whether the music you are listening to is something that would be pleasing to God.

1. Music was in Heaven before the Earth was created.

Ezekiel 28:13 says, *"Thou hast been in Eden the garden of God; every precious stone was thy covering, the sardius, topaz, and the diamond, the beryl, the onyx, and the jasper, the sapphire, the emerald, and the carbuncle, and gold: the workmanship of thy tabrets and of thy pipes was prepared in thee in the day that thou wast created."* This verse is talking about Satan and how God created him. God created him with *"pipes"* which many believe that God was talking about his vocal cords. Satan and the angels he led sang in Heaven before the Earth was ever created.

2. Satan knows more about music than you do.

The fact that God created Satan with the ability to sing reveals the knowledge he has about music. He knows how to influence people with music far better than they realized. Satan has used music to influence more people to go astray from Christ than anything else.

3. Music has always influenced the actions of people.

In the wilderness, the children of Israel sang and danced naked around a golden calf. When Joshua and Moses came down from the mount, Joshua thought he heard the noise of war in the camp. Moses had heard this noise before in Egypt, and he knew this was the sound of the Egyptian music. Moses said in Exodus 32:18 that this was *"the noise of them that sing do I hear."* Israel took the music of Egypt and tried to blend it with their worship of God, and the result was that they ended up dancing naked around a golden calf. This is no doubt the first time we see "Christian rock" in the Scriptures and what it cause people to do.

By the way, it still causes people to go astray from God.

The Book of Psalms is a collection of music that Israel often sang as they either went to the temple, sang around the temple, as they went to war, and when they came home from a war.

Music is very influential in one's life. Satan knows this, the world knows this, and many ignore the negative influence that the wrong music has on them. You show me what type of music you are listening to, and I will show you which direction you are headed spiritually.

4. Music is either spiritual or carnal.

You cannot get caught up in trying to label the genre of music. God calls music either spiritual or carnal. Music is either of the Spirit, or it is of the flesh. Romans 8:7 reminds the believer, *"Because the carnal mind is enmity against God: for it is not subject to the law of*

God, neither indeed can be." If the music you listen to is carnal, it then is at discord with God. The music you listen to influences your walk with Christ. You cannot listen to the wrong music regularly and keep a warm heart toward God.

God is a God of absolutes. There are no gray areas with God. Therefore, the music you listen to is either right or wrong, it is either spiritual or carnal.

5. Spiritual music is divided up into three types:

For the rest of the chapter, I want to focus on Ephesians 5:19, which is one of the greatest verses that defines what God considers spiritual music. This verse says, *"Speaking to yourselves in psalms and hymns and spiritual songs, singing and making melody in your heart to the Lord;"*

Notice that the three types of music defined in this verse are psalms, hymns and spiritual songs. A psalm is music that praises God. The song, "Praise Him, Praise Him" is a great illustration of a psalm. A hymn is music that honors God. The song, "All Hail the Power of Jesus Name" would be considered a hymn. A spiritual song is music that talks about God or truths in His Word. The songs, "Amazing Grace," or "Mansion Over the Hilltop" would be great illustrations of a spiritual song. All spiritual music will fall into one of these categories.

6. There are three parts to music.

Just as there are three type of music, there are also three parts of music. In music you have the lyrics, harmony, and the rhythm. All of these are displayed in Ephesians 5:19. The lyrics, which is the words, would compose the psalms, hymns and spiritual songs. The harmony, is the melody, or the tune you hear when you sing the song. The rhythm is shown when God talks about *"making melody in your heart."* The heart has a rhythm which is a heartbeat. In music you have what many would call the timing, which is the rhythm of the music. All three of these parts of music, if written and played appropriately, will make the believer want to glorify God with all of their being. You must remember that God made man a body, soul and spirit, and spiritual music will cause the believer to want to serve God with their body, soul, and spirit.

7. Spiritual music emphasizes the lyrics over the rhythm.

The words are always to be the most important part of every song. Why? Because the Scriptures are the Word of God. God always places an emphasis on words. When God talks about preserving His Word, He said that He would preserve every word *"from this generation for ever."* Words mean something, and the right music will always emphasize the words. If you only looked at the words of the wrong music without it being sung or hearing the melody or tune, you would find that you would never be stirred to serve the LORD. However, when you read the words of spiritual music, they often stir you to want to serve the LORD. The reason is the words of spiritual music will stir the believer to want to do more for God with their body, soul, and spirit.

8. The melody should always point to the lyrics.

One of the common excuses used by believers in defending their listening to "Christian Rock" and rock music is that they don't listen to the words, but they listen to the music. This argument in itself is wrong. In Ephesians 5:19, God places the emphasis on the words, and not the melody. God is saying that the melody is only the vehicle to carry the words, and the vehicle and the words should be in harmony. Words that talk about the LORD but are carried in the vehicle of the world's sound will produce nothing more than what it did in Israel when they danced around a gold calf; it will produce a carnal believer.

9. The rhythm should never pull away from the lyrics.

The heart is always the destination of music. God warns in Proverbs 4:23, *"Keep thy heart with all diligence; for out of it are the issues of life"* If you are going to keep your heart right with God, you are going to have to listen to the right music that keeps your heart in tune with Him.

The beat in the music should never be the main emphasis. Let me make this clear, every song has a beat. Music that is in 4/4 timing is music that the first note has the beat. It stays in the proper rhythm throughout the rest of the song. The beat doesn't take away from the lyrics or harmony; rather, it compliments them. When the beat become the prominent focus in music is when the flesh becomes the prominent focus of the believer.

Satan often takes the beat and takes it out of the proper rhythm, which results in a change of the heartbeat and can cause the individual to do things that is against the Scriptural principles for how a believer should live.

10. The appearance of songs should always be good.

Romans 14:13 says, *"Let us not therefore judge one another any more: but judge this rather, that no man put a stumblingblock or an occasion to fall in his brother's way."* You have to understand that there is music that reminds some people of their past life in the bars, and any so-called Christian music that would remind people of their previous life in sin becomes a stumblingblock. The music you

101

listen to should never be a stumblingblock, but it should build up those who hear it.

One of the best ways I have learned to judge music is to turn your music on in your car, step out of the car and close the door. When you are outside of the car, you have to ask yourself if that music sounds like spiritual music. If it does not, it is not the right type of music.

My friend, listening to spiritual music will help you to become a spiritual person. Your music is a display of your heart's desires. If you have a desire to please and glorify God with your life, your music will be the type of music that would cause you and others to glorify Him with your life.

CHAPTER ELEVEN

NAKEDNESS

The next two chapters should be read together, as this first chapter is the foundation for the next chapter.

The topic of nakedness and what it is must be dictated by what the Scriptures say, and not by what culture dictates. Just because culture says something is okay doesn't mean that it agrees with the Scriptures. The Scriptures are the final authority on what should dictate how we dress, and how much flesh should be seen.

One may wonder why I would deal with this topic, and the reason I am dealing with this topic is because I am trying to keep the minds of God's people pure. James 1:14 says, *"But every man is tempted, when he is drawn away of his own lust, and enticed."* Seeing someone dressed indecently is inviting the flesh to lust. God would have never addressed this topic in the Scriptures if He didn't want us to define it. God put it in the Scriptures because He wanted to keep your mind pure. So let's dive into this topic and find out why it is so relevant to your life.

WHAT IS NAKEDNESS?

1. Nakedness is showing any of the thigh.

God always used the priests as His standard for clothing. Exodus 28:42 says, *"And thou shalt make them linen breeches to cover their nakedness; from the loins even unto the thighs they shall reach:"* You will notice that from the loins to the kneecap was considered showing your nakedness. In other words, you are not to show your thigh, and this applies to men or women.

2. Nakedness is showing the upper body.

John 21:7 says, *"Therefore that disciple whom Jesus loved saith unto Peter, It is the*

Lord. Now when Simon Peter heard that it was the Lord, he girt his fisher's coat unto him, (for he was naked,) and did cast himself into the sea." Let's use some common sense to define this verse. Peter was fishing, and being completely naked would not make sense. Peter simply had his shirt off while he was fishing. When he saw Jesus, he quickly put his coat or shirt on because he was convicted of not being clothed properly.

When you join these two verses, you realize that anything from the kneecap to the neck is considered nakedness. In other words, you are to keep covered that section of the body with clothing. It doesn't matter how hot it is outside, you are never to see another's nakedness. Only your spouse should be given this privilege. God is very concerned with keeping your mind pure and from temptation, and the only way you are going to do this is to avoid showing your nakedness off to anyone.

STATEMENTS CONCERNING NAKEDNESS

1. Be careful about doing activities that show your nakedness.

Exodus 20:26 says, *"Neither shalt thou go up by steps unto mine altar, that thy nakedness be not discovered thereon."* God wanted the priest to be very careful as to how they walked up the steps onto the altar so that nobody could see their nakedness. If God wanted the priests to be this careful about being decent, I would think that He wants you to be just as careful as well. Be careful in your activities that you are decent at all times.

2. Your sex does not give you an excuse to show off your nakedness.

In Leviticus 18:6-19, God's command to be decent was to both men and women. If it is wrong for a woman to show her nakedness, it is also wrong for a man. It is just as wrong for a man to run around shirtless as it would be for a lady. Your sex doesn't give you a pass on God's command for decency. Both men and women are to be decent at all times.

3. Family is no excuse to show your nakedness.

Leviticus 18:6 says, *"None of you shall approach to any that is near of kin to him, to uncover their nakedness: I am the LORD."* Just because someone is a family member doesn't give you a right to see them indecent. Many young girls have been molested by a brother, dad, or a close family member because the family didn't adhere to decency with each other. You will protect your family from this sin by staying decent with each other.

4. Revealing nakedness causes shame.

Isaiah 47:3 says, *"Thy nakedness shall be uncovered, yea, thy shame shall be seen..."*

Shame is always the end of not being decent. Many people have ruined their mind and their lives because they didn't see the need of covering their nakedness. You cannot expect to stay pure and keep from being controlled by shame if you allow lust to control your mind by seeing indecency.

5. Looking at nakedness always leads to lust and sin.

In 2 Samuel 11:2, you have the story of David committing the great sin of adultery with Bathsheba. However, David's sin of adultery started with lust. He saw her indecent, and that led to adultery. You can't feed the lust of your flesh without eventually succumbing to what your mind has been fed. Many people have believed the lie that they could control their lust only to find that lust controlled them to the point that it ruined their life, relationships, and testimony.

6. **The easiest way not to reveal your nakedness is to stay clothed.**

In Revelation 3:18, God tells this church to be clothed so that the shame of their "*nakedness*" isn't revealed. I know this sound very simple, but if you are always clothed decently, you will never become the source of lust for another. Likewise, if you will keep your eyes from seeing nakedness, you can keep your mind from being fed lustful thoughts.

7. **You keep a pure and innocent mind by staying away from anything that causes you to see that which you should not see.**

God says in 2 Timothy 2:22, "*Flee also youthful lusts...*" There are some things you run from, and one of those things is anything that would feed lust. Let this simple lesson on nakedness be a guide to always dress right, and also a guide on guarding what you allow your eyes to see. If you never see someone dressed indecently, you will never have to be afraid of lust controlling your mind.

CHAPTER TWELVE

PORNOGRAPHY

Psalm 101:3 says, *"I will set no wicked thing before mine eyes: I hate the work of them that turn aside; it shall not cleave to me."* Your eyes are the portal to your mind, and your mind is the battleground where all sin and temptation is fought. This is why God said in 2 Corinthians 10:5, *"Casting down imaginations, and every high thing that exalteth itself against the knowledge of God, and bringing into captivity every thought to the obedience of Christ;"* He knew that if the believer could control what their eyes see, they can control what their mind imagines and thinks. If the eyes have never seen something bad, the mind can never think something wicked. The mind only relies on the information it gets from the eyes.

In the previous chapter, we discussed that the Scriptures teach that nakedness is anything above the knee all the way to the neck. Therefore, if the eyes never see the nakedness of someone, they will never have to fight the evil thoughts of pornography.

Pornography is a multi-billion dollar business. It brings in this much money because of so many people who are addicted to it. They say that approximately seventy percent of men have seen pornography in the past thirty days, and that approximately forty percent of women have also viewed pornography. This is a frightening thing because of what it can do to destroy the minds of God's people. The Scriptures are very clear on the evils of pornography. Let me share with you why pornography is wrong.

1. Pornography is wrong because it feeds the flesh.

Romans 13:14 says, *"But put ye on the Lord Jesus Christ, and make not provision for the* flesh, to fulfil the lusts thereof." God commands the believer not to "make provision" for the flesh. In other words, don't feed your flesh. Your flesh will control you the more you feed it. Pornography only feeds the flesh. You cannot look at it and keep a pure mind. You will never win the battle against the flesh if you allow yourself to view pornography.

2. Pornography is wrong because it pollutes the mind.

2 Corinthians 10:5 says, "Casting down imaginations, and every high thing that exalteth itself against the knowledge of God, and bringing into captivity every thought to the obedience of Christ;" Pornography has a way of causing your mind to think wicked thoughts; thoughts that you would never think about if you never viewed it. God says in the verse above that you are to bring into "captivity every thought to the obedience of Christ." There is no way you will accomplish

113

this if you view pornography because it will control you instead of you controlling your mind.

3. Pornography is wrong because it creates temptation.

James 1:14 says, *"But every man is tempted, when he is drawn away of his own lust, and enticed."* Temptation is created when a person allows their lust to entice them. Pornography's purpose is to feed your lust; therefore, you can't help but fight temptation of sin if you allow yourself to view pornography.

4. Pornography is wrong because it promotes impurity.

Philippians 4:8 says, *"Finally, brethren, whatsoever things are true, whatsoever things are honest, whatsoever things are just, WHATSOEVER THINGS ARE PURE, whatsoever things are lovely, whatsoever* things are of good report; if there be any virtue, and if there be any praise, think on these things." Now, let me ask you, can you honestly say that you can look at pornography and never have an impure thought? You cannot obey Philippians 4:8 and look at pornography at the same time.

5. Pornography is wrong because it turns people into objects.

Genesis 1:27 says, "So God created man in his own image, in the image of God created he him; male and female created he them." Ladies are not objects, but they are humans whom God has created. One of the main problems with pornography is that it makes a man to look at a woman as an object instead of a human. When a person is addicted to pornography, they look at every person of the opposite sex as an opportunity with whom they can fulfill their lust. One of the reasons men who look at pornography often have an anger issue is because "their object" is not doing what they imagined in their mind; therefore, they become angry with people. In a Spirit-controlled mind, you won't look at people as objects, but as individuals who God has created for His purpose.

6. Pornography is wrong because it controls the individual.

When you read Romans 7:7-25, you will see a person who is controlled by sin to the point of despair. Pornography will control you to the point that nobody will ever please you. One of the reasons pornography is wrong is because it is controlling you instead of the Holy Spirit controlling you.

7. Pornography is wrong because it destroys relationships and families.

You can't build a good relationship when your relationship is built on lust. Likewise, you won't keep good relationships when they are built on lust. You will find yourself becoming a lonely person if you allow yourself to be controlled by the sin of pornography.

HOW DO YOU OVERCOME PORNOGRAPHY?

1. Flee opportunities to feed this sin.

1 Corinthians 6:18 says, "Flee fornication..." There are some sins you will be able to fight against, but there are other sins that will control you to the point that the only way to defeat them is by running from them. In other words, you must get away from anything that would feed that sin. Pornography is one of those sins from which you must flee. You should treat pornography as if it were a deadly poison.

The three devices that will feed you pornography are television, cell phone, and the computer. My friend, be very careful when you are on these devices that you don't allow yourself to go to places where you can feed this sin. Satan is sly, and he will use these things in a weak moment to continue to control you through the sin of pornography.

2. Read and memorize God's Word.

Psalm 119:9 say, *"Wherewithal shall a young man cleanse his way? by taking heed thereto according to thy word."* God's Word is like a bar of soap for the mind. The more you feed your mind God's Word, the more you will wash your mind of impure thoughts. My advice would be to read large quantities of God's Word, and memorize large portions of Scripture.

3. Avoid conversations that lead to impure thoughts.

When you see a conversation starting to go in a direction that will lead to impure thoughts, you must quickly get away from that conversation. Whether the conversation is in person, or it is done through talking immorally through text or phone apps, you must avoid these portals that will lead you to wanting to feed your mind more of this immoral sin.

4. Yield to the Holy Spirit.

When you are yielded to the Holy Spirit, the flesh will have to die. Several times throughout the day you must pray to the Holy Spirit, and yield yourself to Him in that prayer. When you begin to fight the urge to look at something wrong, pray and ask the Holy Spirit to help you to overcome that thought. You cannot be yielded to the Holy Spirit and do wrong at the same time.

5. Be accountable to someone.

Most people are going to need someone to whom they are accountable. You need to

119

weekly talk to your accountability partner and let them know how you are doing. By the way, that person to whom you are accountable needs to be a spiritual person. The worst thing you can do is to make a peer your accountability partner. Your pastor is most likely the best person from whom you can get help and be accountable to with this evil sin. You can overcome the lust of pornography, but it will only be done with help from someone who will hold you accountable for your actions.

CHAPTER THIRTEEN

PROPER SPEECH

When I was a boy, we were taught never to take God's name in vain. If we ever took God's name in vain, my parents would take a bar soap and wash our mouth out with soap. Oh, I have found myself with that bar soap in my mouth. I remember one time after I got home from school that I started to say a word that my parents taught us not to say. In the middle of the word I caught myself and I changed what I was saying. The problem, my mother caught that I had changed that word and she ended up taking me into the restroom to wash my mouth out with soap. I promise you, that word has never come out of my mouth again because of how my mother made it important not to say such words.

To the Jews, the name of God was so holy that the Jew never mentioned His name in fear that they would be killed. The reason they feared His name was because they were taught that His name was holy. There are times in the Scriptures when some of God's names were so revered that they were afraid to say it because they were afraid they would be killed if they said God's name.

Times have certainly changed. Curse words have become a part of most conversations. There used to be a day when people would blush or were embarrassed when someone cursed. Sadly, we live in a society when the words that come from many mouths is almost crude and embarrassing. I can remember a day when a lady never spoke a curse word; compare that to today's world when they speak just as vile as many men. Sadly, we have gotten used to cursing which has corrupted our nation. If there is ever an area where we need a revival, it is in this area of learning how to speak properly. Let me give you a few thoughts about what the Scripture says about how we should speak.

1. God's name is holy.

Psalm 111:9 says, *"He sent redemption unto his people: he hath commanded his covenant for ever: holy and reverend is his name."* The word *"holy"* means sacred, revered, or set aside. God expects His name to be so sacred that we don't use it in a vile manner. Let me make this very clear, God's name is not a curse word. Let me go further to say, that the name of Jesus Christ is also not a curse word. God's name is to be holy, set aside, and in such a manner that nobody would even think of using His name as a curse word.

2. God's name is not to be used in vain.

Exodus 20:7 says, *"Thou shalt not take the name of the LORD thy God in vain; for the LORD will not hold him guiltless that taketh his name in vain."* God expects His name not to be used in vain. I'm afraid that too many people are so flippant in how they use God's name. For instance, I do not believe that it is right for people to say, "Oh my God." When you use statements like this, you are taking God's name in vain. Moreover, I also believe that we should not use the name "Jesus" as a curse word. Jesus name is the name by which we are saved, and it is not a name that we should use as a swear word or a curse word when we are frustrated. Let me repeat that God does not expect us to use His name as a swear word or in a vain manner.

3. Minced oaths are just as wrong as the real word.

Nehemiah 13:24 says, *"And their children spake half in the speech of Ashdod, and could not speak in the Jews' language, but according to the language of each people."* The sad part about these people is that their

124

speech was half in the Jews' language and half in Ashdod's language. In other words, they minced their words so that you could not discern the bad words from the good words.

A minced oath is a form of cursing that replaces a direct curse word with a "better sounding word" which in effect is still cursing. You may recall at the beginning of this chapter how I talked about my mom washing my mouth out with soap. The reason she washed my mouth out with soap was because I used one of these minced oaths. There are several words that we use today that are nothing more than curse words that are camouflaged in a minced oath. The following is a few of the minced oaths that I am talking about.

"Gee" — mid 19th century: an abbreviation of Jesus.

"Golly" — late 18th century: euphemism for God.

"Gosh" — mid 18th century: euphemism for God.

James 3:2 says, *"For in many things we offend all. If any man offend not in word, the same is a perfect man, and able also to bridle the whole body."* You should hold your tongue in such a manner that none of these words would ever come from your mouth.

4. Your language should represent your God.

Psalm 19:14 says, *"Let the words of my mouth, and the meditation of my heart, be acceptable in thy sight, O LORD, my strength, and my redeemer."* Everything you say should be something that God would not be ashamed or angry with you speaking. I often say to people that they must be so careful that they would only let come from their mouths what they would say before God.

There have been times when somebody apologizes to me for allowing a curse word to slip from their lips because I'm a pastor. Let me make this clear, just because I'm a pastor doesn't mean somebody should guard their language. They should guard their language because God always hears every word that comes from your mouth. Everything you say should be something that God would not be ashamed or angry of hearing.

For instance, I don't believe that we should be talking about body parts in an open conversation. Talking about private body parts is not glorifying to God. I believe the believer must be so careful not to describe a body part because that would not be a good representative as a believer. Your private conversations should be as holy as how you would speak in public. If you wouldn't talk about body parts in public, neither should you talk about them in private.

127

5. How you speak represents who you spend time with.

You can always tell where a person lives by the way that they talk. When you go down south, you will hear people talk with a Southern drawl. When you go up to the Northeast, you will find that many times they will not pronounce "r" in their words. You can always tell where a person is from by the how they talk.

God says in Matthew 12:35-37, *"A good man out of the good treasure of the heart bringeth forth good things: and an evil man out of the evil treasure bringeth forth evil things. But I say unto you, That every idle word that men shall speak, they shall give account thereof in the day of judgment. For by thy words thou shalt be justified, and by thy words thou shalt be condemned."* Can I ask you, how can a believer allow curse words to come from your mouth? How you speak represents with

128

whom you were spending time. There are several words that should never be a part of your conversation. For instance: D-a-m-n, H-e-l-l, H-e-c-k, D-a-n-g, S-u-c-k-s, or C-r-a-p should never come from your lips. These words come from the world, and should not be a part of the believer's conversation.

6. Angry or belittling words should not be a part of the Christian conversation.

Things you say about people should be graceful. Ephesians 4:29 say, *"Let no corrupt communication proceed out of your mouth, but that which is good to the use of edifying, that it may minister grace unto the hearers."* Just because you are angry doesn't give you a right to say hateful or rude things to people. Be very careful about the words that you say. The little phrase, "Sticks and stones may break my bones, but words will never harm me" is a lie. Words do hurt. What you say does matter. I am saying that the Christian must be careful not to belittle someone else. Let me remind you that the person you are belittling is the creation of God. Do you understand that God made them that way? Do you understand that God will hold you accountable for what you say about others? God will not hold you guiltless when you belittle people and speak in an angry manner because you are out of control. Just because you are angry doesn't give you a right to curse, or swear, or to belittle others.

7. Be proper in your speech.

Let me caution you about watering down the word with today's slang. God wants the believer to speak properly. Proverbs 25:11 says, *"A word fitly spoken is like apples of gold in pictures of silver."* God is saying that He expects His children to be proper in their speech. I believe one of the ways that Satan destroys a society is by destroying their speech. Let me caution you about using slang words; instead, just say what you are supposed to say and in the manner that God would want you to say it.

8. Everything you say should be acceptable to God.

Words are important, and every word should be spoken to show that you are a child of God. Psalm 19:14 says, *"Let the words of my mouth, and the meditation of my heart, be acceptable in thy sight, O LORD, my strength, and my redeemer."* Everything that you say should be acceptable to God. Let me encourage you to guard the words that you speak, and be so guarded with your words that you would make sure that what comes from your mouth would be acceptable to God if He was physically present when you are talking.

CHAPTER FOURTEEN

THE RIGHT FRIENDS

Your friends will have more to do with who you become in life more than anything else. Many times we never think about how much our friends influence us; however, every person who lived right has done right because they were influenced by the right friends.

My wife and I were talking about some of the friends who we went to school with, and as we discussed different people, we thought about what they became as adults. As we looked at different people who had gone the wrong way in life, we always found that the common denominator was their friends. They all had at least one friend who didn't do right, and that one friend influenced them for wrong.

We have to realize that we are only as strong as our weakest friend. Whoever is your weakest friend is how strong you will be in life.

You cannot expect to be strong as a believer with weak friends. Your friends influence your thinking, associations, and the direction in life you take. Your friends dictate who you marry, and oftentimes dictate what you do for the LORD. If you want to keep your life spiritually on track for God, you need to make sure that all of your friends are the right type of friends.

2 Samuel 13:1-3 says, *"And it came to pass after this, that Absalom the son of David had a fair sister, whose name was Tamar; and Amnon the son of David loved her. And Amnon was so vexed, that he fell sick for his sister Tamar; for she was a virgin; and Amnon thought it hard for him to do any thing to her. But Amnon had a friend, whose name was Jonadab, the son of Shimeah David's brother: and Jonadab was a very subtil man."* The one thing that the Scriptures teach us about Amnon was that he had at least one bad friend. You notice about Amnon that it wasn't the amount of friends

that he had; it was that he had one friend who was bad. Amnon could have had 100 friends, but it was the one friend who ended up giving him an evil plan to do something bad with his sister. If one bad friend destroyed Amnon, you had best be careful about the friends you choose.

HOW DO YOU IDENTIFY BAD FRIENDS?

1. They always run in a crowd.

The one thing that you always see about bad friends is that they cannot stand by themselves. Bad friends thrive in groups, and avoid being alone. They normally have no confidence in themselves; in fact, most of the time their boldness and confidence comes from the power they get when they are with their bad friends. If you catch a bad friend by themselves, they are normally not as bold as they would be if they were with their friends.

2. They always point to themselves and not authority.

One of the great identifiers of bad friends is that they will talk bad about your parents, your preacher, the police, and any type of authority. The wrong friends will try to pull you away from the authorities in your life instead of trying to push you towards them because they want you to make them your authority.

3. They don't do things publicly.

Bad friends don't openly tell you about their intentions. The Bible talks about Amnon's friend being very subtil. The wrong type of friends will try to influence you to do something wrong that you would not do if they didn't influence you. It is their intention to try to get you to do wrong. They are subtil or smooth as a snake in their influence to get you to do wrong.

When I think of bad friends, I think of Satan who is very subtle in his moves. Satan is never open about his intentions; likewise, the wrong type of friends are never open about their intentions of their friendship with you. Most of the time, the wrong type of friends will try in private to get you to do something in public that they are not willing to do.

4. They turn you from your heritage.

Bad friends criticize the past as being out of touch and out of date. You can always identify a bad friend by how they look at your heritage. If you have a good friend, they will embrace your heritage that has been given to you by your parents, and by God's Word.

5. They try to get you believe that you are your own authority.

An identifying characteristic about bad friends is that they try to persuade you that you are your own authority. A bad friend doesn't believe in authority; in fact, they try to persuade you that you are your own authority. My friend, everybody has to have authority. It doesn't matter who you are, your last name, or who your parents are, you must have authorities in your life.

HOW DO I CHOOSE FRIENDS?

1. Let everyone know your direction.

When you let everybody know what your direction is in life, you will find that you will ward off the wrong type of friends, and discover good friends. When I was a teenager, I let everybody know that my desire in life was to be a preacher. What that did for me was that it kept the wrong girls away from me, and it kept me from the wrong friends. You can save yourself from the heartache of the wrong friends by simply declaring that you plan on serving God with the rest of your life.

2. Make right authority your heroes.

Your heroes dictate who you will become. When you make men of God or godly ladies your heroes, depending on what sex you are, you are telling everybody that you want to go the right way in life. I'm always hesitant about people whose heroes are sports stars, Hollywood stars, or rock music musicians. Making the right authority your heroes is vital to you having the right friends.

3. Choose friends from the right places.

Some of the right places to choose your friends from are church and soul winning time. The bad friends won't want to be in church. The bad friends won't want to go to Sunday school. You will find friends of a lifetime who will help you to serve the LORD by choosing your friends as you do right. You'll never find the right friends in a bar or at a rock concert. You find good friends in church, and you can find good friends by working in bus ministry of your local church.

4. Choose friends with a right direction.

Choose the type of friends who love authority. The direction that your friends have will dictate what direction you go. If you have friends who love authorities, and you love authority, you will find that both you and your friends will go the right way in life. Likewise, if you choose friends who have declared that they want to serve God, you will find that both you and your friends will go the right direction in life. When I was young man, I had friends who all wanted to serve God for their entire life. My friends as a teenage young man were friends who had the desire to serve the LORD full-time. One of the reasons why I turned out right is not because I was a super Christian; it was because I had friends who wanted to serve God.

Moreover, choose friends who have the same type of fire that you have. Choose the friends who want to sit up front in church and are excited about serving the LORD. Choose your friends by how much they get excited about the preaching of God's Word and souls being saved. Your friends will dictate what you eventually become.

5. Make most of your friends older people.

Another reason I turned out right is because most of my friends were older people. You will do yourself a great favor by making older Christians your friends. Older people may not be as exciting as your peers, but older people will want you to do what is right and will guard you against the wrong crowd. There is nothing wrong with having friends who are your age, but it would better if you have friends who are older and have been through life, who know what life tries to do to you. Older people you want to be friends with may not run to you for friendship, but spend time around them and become friends to them. You will find that they will be a great deterrent to the bad people who will attempt to get you not to serve the LORD.

6. Choose friends that are stronger than you.

Proverbs 27:17 says, *"Iron sharpeneth iron; so a man sharpeneth the countenance of his friend."* If you choose friends who are stronger than you, they will pull you up to where they live. However, if you choose friends who are weaker than you, they will likely pull you down to do the same bad level of sin that they are doing. Make sure that your friends are stronger than you.

7. Choose friends with common goals.

Choose your friends who have the same goals and determination to serve the LORD. If

141

your goal is to serve the LORD in full-time service, choose friends who have that same goal. You both have a common goal of serving the LORD full-time, it will help you to keep serving the LORD.

Your friends do matter. Having the right friends will determine how long you serve the LORD. Let me challenge you to let this list that I have given you guide you in how you choose friends.

CHAPTER FIFTEEN

SMOKING AND DRUGS

Romans 6:12-14 says, *"Let not sin therefore reign in your mortal body, that ye should obey it in the lusts thereof. Neither yield ye your members as instruments of unrighteousness unto sin: but yield yourselves unto God, as those that are alive from the dead, and your members as instruments of righteousness unto God. For sin shall not have dominion over you: for ye are not under the law, but under grace."* When God says, *"Let not sin therefore reign in your mortal body,"* He is saying that the believer is not to come under the control of anything. In other words, you are not to be addicted to anything. One of the greatest reasons drugs, alcohol, and smoking are wrong is because they are all addictive.

One of the nastiest habits that anyone can acquire is the habit of smoking. Smoking is a nervous habit, and those who smoke don't realize how much it stinks. You will often find that when smokers get nervous, they tend to grab for a cigarette because it tends to pacify what is going on in their life. The problem with this mindset is that you're trusting a cigarette for peace instead of trusting God.

Drugs is no better; not because of the smell are drugs bad, even though drugs can at times smell bad, but it is because of what drugs do to your body. Your body belongs to God. When looking at the Scriptures, you will find out that they show that smoking and drugs are a sin. Let me share with you several reasons why smoking and drugs are bad.

1. Your body belongs to God.

1 Corinthians 6:19 says, *"What? know ye not that your body is the temple of the Holy Ghost which is in you, which ye have of God, and ye are not your own?"* Smoking and drugs

are wrong because of what you are doing to your body. Each of these vices damage your body. Once you get saved, your body no longer belongs to you; therefore, you have no right to abuse your body with drugs and cigarettes because you are abusing the temple of the Holy Ghost.

If I were to ask you to give a cigarette to the Holy Spirit to smoke, would you do it? If Jesus Christ were in your presence, would you force a cigarette into His mouth or put drugs in his veins without His agreement? You absolutely would not do that. You know that it would be wrong to do such. Now let me ask you, what do you think you are doing when you smoke cigarettes or take drugs? You are putting those drugs and that cigarette into the face of the God who lives inside of your heart. Smoking and drugs are wrong because your body belongs to God and you have no right to do with your body what you want to do with it.

2. Smoking and drugs makes you a servant to sin.

Romans 6:14 says, *"For sin shall not have dominion over you: for ye are not under the law, but under grace."* You have to understand that God does not want the believer to be under the control of anything or anybody else other than His Holy Spirit. When you smoke or take drugs, you are becoming a servant to these vices. Many become so controlled by these vices that they are a servant to it. In other words, they will do whatever it takes to satisfy the urge for the vice.

3. Only the Holy Spirit is to control you.

Ephesians 5:18 says, *"And be not drunk with wine, wherein is excess; but be filled with the Spirit;"* The only one who is to control the believer is the Holy Spirit of God. For you to let anything or anyone else to control you other than the Holy Spirit is sin. Smoking and doing drugs is not something that the Holy Spirit would do. You are in direct disobedience to God when you partake of any of these vices.

4. Smoking and drugs hinders your testimony for God.

1 Corinthians 4:9 says, *"For I think that God hath set forth us the apostles last, as it were appointed to death: for we are made a spectacle unto the world, and to angels, and to men."* Smoking and drugs hurts your testimony and the ability to help others to get saved.

I heard a story recently of a young believer who was trying to invite people to church, when they asked a lost person if they could bum a cigarette off them, one of the people watching said, "I didn't know that church people did that." The person who was with this young believer explained, "This person is a brand new Christian, and they are just learning how to live the Christian life." What did their desire to smoke do? This hurt that person's ability to be a testimony for Jesus Christ. If the only reason you should give up smoking is to help your testimony so you can better reach people for Jesus Christ, that in itself should motivate you to quit smoking.

5. Smoking and drugs shortens your ability to serve God because it's bad for your health.

Ecclesiastes 7:17 says, *"Be not over much wicked, neither be thou foolish: why shouldest thou die before thy time?"* God is saying that we have to be careful about doing anything that would cause us to shorten our life. Proverbs 10:27 says, *"The fear of the LORD prolongeth days: but the years of the wicked shall be shortened."* God wants us to live our life in such a way that we don't do things that would shorten it. Smoking and drugs will

148

absolutely shorten your life. Many people have had their life shortened because of their addiction to cigarettes or drugs.

6. Smoking and drugs wastes God's money on sin.

Proverbs 23:5 says, *"Wilt thou set thine eyes upon that which is not? for riches certainly make themselves wings; they fly away as an eagle toward heaven."* God has always commanded the believer to be very careful about how they spend money. You cannot spend money on cigarettes and drugs and say that that is how God wants you to spend His money. Please understand that the money you have is God's money in the first place. For you to take that money and spend it on a vice that will destroy your testimony and your ability to serve God is not something that He would spend His money on; therefore, wasting God's money on vices is a sin.

7. Smoking and drugs identifies you with the world.

Galatians 5:1 says, *"Stand fast therefore in the liberty wherewith Christ hath made us free, and be not entangled again with the yoke of bondage."* Before you were saved is when you got entangled in the vices of the world. Let me ask you, why would you get entangled again in the life that you came out of when you got saved? The worst thing you can do is go back to the same old life you used to live before you got saved. The life you used to live led to bondage. Why would you want to go back to the same bondage?

8. Smoking and drugs hurts others.

Matthew 7:12 says, *"Therefore all things whatsoever ye would that men should do to you, do ye even so to them: for this is the law and the prophets."* When you smoke cigarettes or do drugs, you are hurting those around you. Second-hand smoke from cigarettes is well-known to hurt the health of others. The drugs you take will take money out of the mouths of children, and at times, they can cause you to do things that can physically hurt others. One reason you should never smoke or do drugs is just because it can cause you to hurt the ones you love and the innocent people who have nothing to do with your sin.

9. These habits teach others to have bad habits.

Romans 14:13 says, *"Let us not therefore judge one another any more: but judge this rather, that no man put a stumblingblock or an occasion to fall in his brother's way."* If the only reason that smoking and drugs are wrong is because it is going to hurt your ability to help others. That of itself should cause you to understand that it is a sin. If smoking would be a stumblingblock for somebody not to get saved, or for somebody not to want to serve

151

the LORD, that should cause you to quit smoking. If doing drugs would cause someone to stumble spiritually, and it will, you should stop doing drugs. Anything you do that would hurt another person's ability to serve the LORD should be avoided at all cost.

My friend, you know inside of your heart that smoking and drugs are wrong; however, it really doesn't matter what you know is right or wrong, the fact that God's Word says it is wrong makes it wrong. When you choose to smoke or take drugs, you are choosing to rebel against God.

Never allow yourself to get caught up in these bad habits. The best way to avoid these bad habits is never to do them the first time. If there's never a first time of smoking or doing drugs, there will never be a second time. Stay clean from cigarettes and drugs; you will never regret it.

CHAPTER SIXTEEN

TATTOOS AND CUTTING

Tattooing is a 1.5 billion dollar business in the United States. It used to be that getting a tattoo was look down upon, but now it has become a fad in our modern culture. Before you would see people get one or two tattoos on their body, now you have people who have marked their body up so much that you could barely see any part of their skin because of the tattoos. It is a sad day that so many believers see nothing wrong with getting a tattoo. One thing to remember is that the further we get from God the more that people will mark up their body.

There are several reasons why the Scripture forbids cutting and tattoos. Before I get into the main portion of this lesson, let me just remind you that when you look at heathen societies, you will see them cut themselves and mark their bodies with ink to identify with their tribes and false gods. As God's children, we must realize that we belong to God. Our body does not belong to us because it is the temple of the Holy Ghost. Because our body is the temple of the Holy Ghost, we should treat it the same way that God would want us to treat Him. So, why are tattoos and cutting wrong?

1. It is forbidden by God.

Leviticus 19:28 says, *"Ye shall not make any cuttings in your flesh for the dead, nor print any marks upon you: I am* **the LORD***."* The very first reason why it is wrong is because God forbids it. God knew that these marks upon the bodies were to identify them with false gods, and the believer is only to be identified with one person, and that is Jesus Christ.

2. It is equated with paganism and Satanism.

Mark 5:5 says, *"And always, night and day, he was in the mountains, and in the tombs, crying, and cutting himself with stones."* This verse is talking about a young man who was possessed with devils and was cutting himself. If cutting is so right, why would God mention this in a negative way? The reason why He mentions it in a negative way is because it is wrong.

1 Kings 18:28 says, *"And they cried aloud, and cut themselves after their manner with knives and lancets, till the blood gushed out upon them."* This is the story about Elijah challenging the prophets of Baal. The prophets of Baal, trying to call on their god cut themselves until their blood gushed out with hope that he would respond to their plea. As we know, Baal did not answer their plea because he is not a real God; he is a false god.

As God's people, why would we copy a heathen religion. As God's people, we should treat our body in such a way that the heathen religions would look at how we live and how we treat our body with such respect that they know something is different about us.

3. It is not your body to do with it what you want.

1 Corinthians 3:16-17 says, *"Know ye not that ye are the temple of God, and that the Spirit of God dwelleth in you? If any man defile the temple of God, him shall God destroy; for the temple of God is holy, which temple ye are."* It is very clear in the Scriptures that your body is the temple of the Holy Ghost. God makes it very obvious that the person who defiles God's temple will be destroyed. If you want to be blessed by God as a believer, you cannot practice the heathen ways and expect Him to bless your life. God expects the

156

believer to treat his body in a sacred manner because it belongs to Him.

4. It dishonors the body that God gave you.

Romans 1:24 says, *"Wherefore God also gave them up to uncleanness through the lusts of their own hearts, to dishonour their own bodies between themselves:"* The Scriptures makes it very clear that we are not to dishonor our body. We already know that marking the body is a tradition of false religions, so to mark it up would be to dishonor the very body that God gave you. Again, you have no right to do with your body what you want to do because it belongs to God.

5. It destroys the temple of God.

2 Corinthians 6:16 says, *"And what agreement hath the temple of God with idols? for ye are the temple of the living God; as God hath*

said, I will dwell in them, and walk in them; and I will be their God, and they shall be my people." Whenever you mark your body with a tattoo, you are destroying the temple of God. How do you think that you can represent God the way that you're supposed to when you have destroyed the very temple with which He gives you to serve Him. Tattoos or cutting your body is a purposeful act to destroy the temple that God has given you to serve Him with.

6. It identifies you with worldliness.

Deuteronomy 14:1 says, "Ye are the children of the LORD your God: ye shall not cut yourselves, nor make any baldness between your eyes for the dead." God says you are to come out from the world, not go to the world to be like it. God makes it clear that when you do things that identify you with the world that it's wrong. The Scriptures are clear that tattoos and cutting simply identifies you with the world that you are not to be a partaker of as a believer.

7. It is addictive.

1 Corinthians 6:12 says, *"All things are lawful unto me, but all things are not expedient: all things are lawful for me, <u>but I will not be brought under the power of any.</u>"* Many have said that tattooing becomes very addictive. My friend, you are not to do anything that can control you and cause you to do things that are against God's will. If tattooing can become addictive, and it has been proven that it does, you as a believer should instead yield to the Holy Spirit and not to the desire of the flesh to go get a tattoo.

8. Your motive for a tattoo is not to glorify God, but to please yourself.

1 Corinthians 6:19-20 says, *"What? know ye not that your body is the temple of the Holy*

159

Ghost which is in you, which ye have of God, and ye are not your own? For ye are bought with a price: therefore glorify God in your body, and in your spirit, which are God's. " Your motive in life should always be to glorify God. The fact that you would get a tattoo for your own desires and not to glorify God tells you that it is a sin.

1 Corinthians 10:31 says, "Whether therefore ye eat, or drink, or whatsoever ye do, do all to the glory of God." Everything a believer does should be done to glorify God. My friend, you belong to God. Your purpose in life is to glorify Him. If tattooing and cutting would cause you not to glorify God, you should never allow yourself to have one tattoo on your body.

9. It is a waste of God's money.

The expense that it cost to get a tattoo is expensive. I did a small research on the cost of the average tattoo. Below are the findings that I found.

Tiny Tattoo (Under 2 in) — $30 – $100

Small Tattoo (2 - 4 in) — $50 – $250

Medium Tattoo (4 - 6 in) — $150 – $450

Large Tattoo (6+ in) — $500 – $4,000

Why would you waste your money on something that would make you look so ugly, and that will also cause you to dishonor the temple that God has given for you to serve Him? Don't waste the money that God has given you on such a wicked sin.

10. It hurts your ability to have a pure testimony.

1 Corinthians 10:23 says, *"All things are lawful for me, but all things are not expedient: all things are lawful for me, but all things edify not."* The one thing that a tattoo hurts the most is your ability to have a good testimony

161

for Jesus Christ. Picture one day your body lying in a casket, people walking by and looking at the tattoos that you got printed on your body; tattoos that represent the lifestyle of the world and cutting marks that represent times of self-absorption. How would that be a testimony for Christ? My friend, you hurt your testimony when you're marked up with the world. This chapter is not about maligning those who got tattoos before they got saved. This chapter is about warning the believer about getting more tattoos after they get saved. It doesn't matter if you tattoo a cross on your body to identify with the crucifixion of Christ, it is still against God's Word. Let me encourage you to stay away from this modern fad of tattooing. One day you'll regret the fact that you cannot take off the tattoos that you should have never gotten. Keep your body clean from the tattoos of the world, and you will never have regrets about getting them one day when you become old.

CHAPTER SEVENTEEN

TITHING

Tithing is one of the greatest revealers of your heart. God knows where your heart is by whether you're willing to obey Him in this area of tithing. Show me a person who is not tithing and I will show you a person who is not right with God. Show me a person who is tithing, and I will show you a person who God is blessing their finances.

Tithing is not to be done because we agree with it, tithing is done because God commands it. Tithing is more than just an Old Testament command, tithing is a command that is also found in the New Testament. Just because tithing is mainly mentioned in the Old Testament does not mean that God doesn't want the believer to tithe. We often get caught up in the argument about it being in the Old Testament, but all of the Ten Commandments are in the Old Testament as well. Do we not obey the Ten Commandments because they are in the Old Testament? Absolutely not! We obey all of God's Word because it is all God's Word. Only people with a greedy heart will balk at preaching on tithing.

In the Scriptures, we find that there are several principles about the command of tithing and why it is Scriptural.

1. God commands every believer to tithe.

Malachi 3:10 says, *"Bring ye all the tithes into the storehouse, that there may be meat in mine house, and prove me now herewith, saith the LORD of hosts, if I will not open you the windows of heaven, and pour you out a blessing, that there shall not be room enough to receive it."* When God says bring all the tithes into the storehouse, this is not a choice, but it is a command. You are to tithe because God commands you to tithe.

164

2. You are to tithe to the local church.

Malachi 3:10 says, *"Bring ye all the tithes into the storehouse…"* The important word in this verse is the word *"storehouse."* What is the storehouse? 1 Corinthians 16:1 shows us when it says, *"Now concerning the collection for the saints, as I have given order to the churches of Galatia, even so do ye. Upon the first day of the week let every one of you lay by him in store, as God hath prospered him, that there be no gatherings when I come."* As you can see from these verses, the store is the local church. In other words, God expects you to give your tithe to your local church. Giving money to an outside organization is not tithing because you can only tithe to a local church.

3. Tithing is giving 10% of your income.

The word tithe means tenth. In other words, God is saying that if you are going to tithe, you are supposed to give 10% of your gross income to God. The easy way to figure out 10% is by moving the decimal point over one number to the left of your gross income, and this will show you how much you should tithe. For sake of illustration, if you earned $100, you move the decimal point over one space to the left which leaves you giving God $10. This is the easy way to see how much you should tithe.

4. You should tithe because Jesus said to tithe.

Matthew 23:23 says, *"Woe unto you, scribes and Pharisees, hypocrites! for ye pay tithe of mint and anise and cummin, and have omitted the weightier matters of the law, judgment, mercy, and faith: **these ought ye to have done, and not to leave the other undone**."* So, what is it that you should not leave undone, or what is it that we should have done? God is saying we should pay tithe. In other words, it is not just an Old Testament

166

command to tithe, but we see Jesus in the New Testament commanding people to tithe. Tithing is a command found throughout the Scriptures.

5. You should tithe because the Patriarchs tithed.

Hebrew 7:5-6 says, *"And verily they that are of the sons of Levi, who receive the office of the priesthood, have a commandment to take tithes of the people according to the law, that is, of their brethren, though they come out of the loins of Abraham: But he whose descent is not counted from them received tithes of Abraham, and blessed him that had the promises."* If the Patriarchs tithed, certainly their example should motivate you to tithe. Understand that the Scriptures say that Jesus Christ is the same yesterday, today, and forever; therefore, if God commanded the Patriarchs to tithe, His command has not changed for those of us who live in the New Testament age.

167

6. You should tithe because it shows your heart towards God.

Matthew 6:21 says, *"For where your treasure is, there will your heart be also."* You can always tell where a person's heart is by where they give their money. You cannot say that your heart is with God and hold back your tithe. Tithing is a great revealer of your heart. People who struggle spiritually are people who struggle with their tithing. A person who wants to get right with God always want to be right with their finances. Wherever you invest your money reveals where you have placed your heart.

7. You should tithe because you want God's favor.

Malachi 3:8 says, *"Will a man rob God? Yet ye have robbed me. But ye say, Wherein have we robbed thee? In tithes and offerings."* There is a difference between robbing

168

someone and burglarizing them. To burglarize someone means you stole something from them without them being there. Robbing someone means you put someone's life at risk by threat to get something from them that does not belong to you. When God said we robbed Him, He is saying that we are trying to take back that which belongs to God by threatening Him. My friend, you will never get in God's favor by threatening Him. One of the quickest ways to get on God's bad side is to rob Him of His money.

8. You should tithe because you want God's blessings.

Malachi 3:10 says, *"Bring ye all the **tithes** into the storehouse, that there may be meat in mine house, and prove me now herewith, saith the LORD of hosts, if I will not open you the windows of heaven, and **pour you out a blessing**, that there shall not be room enough to receive it."* God is daring you to test Him in

169

this area of tithing. God says if you will tithe that He will pour you out a blessing. God didn't just say a blessing, but he said *"that there shall not be room enough to receive it."* God is promising you that you will never be able to out-give Him.

9. You should tithe so that you keep from being cursed.

Malachi 3:9 says, *"Ye are cursed with a curse: for ye have robbed me..."* When a person doesn't tithe, they can be guaranteed that everything they touch is going to be cursed by God. If you don't want God to curse everything you touch, then you would be wise to continue to obey God and tithe.

10. You should tithe so that your prayers can be answered.

Malachi 3:10 says, *"Bring ye all the tithes into the storehouse, that there may be meat in mine house, and prove me now herewith, saith the LORD of hosts, if I will not open you the windows of heaven, and pour you out a blessing..."* When God talks about opening the windows of Heaven, He is talking about answering your prayers. You would be wise to tithe if you want your prayers to be answered. Why? Because tithing puts you in favor with God. When you're in God's favor, you're going to find that it is easier to get your prayers answered in time of need.

So my question to you is this; do you want to stay in favor with God? Do you want God's blessings on your life? Do you want God to bless your finances? My advice to you would be to obey God's command to tithe if you want these blessings on your life.

CHAPTER EIGHTEEN

ACTING IN CHURCH

Psalm 101:2 says, *"I will behave myself wisely in a perfect way. O when wilt thou come unto me? I will walk within my house with a perfect heart."* When God says, *"I will behave myself wisely in a perfect way,"* He is saying that we will act mature in His house. The word *"perfect"* is the same word we use as mature. God is saying that how we behave will eventually come from how we act in His house. The words *"my house"* is talking about the church house. In other words, God is saying that when we go to church, we are to act right or mature and behave ourselves in church. He is saying that we are to do everything we can in our power to make sure that we behave properly in church.

As a child, I've always been taught to behave right in church. I cannot remember a time when I acted as some people do in church. I believe too many times we react in church to everybody else's behavior and we end up misbehaving when we go to church. It is important for the preaching of the Word of God for people to behave right when they go to church. It is important for people being saved that everyone does what they're supposed to do when they come to church. I believe for the sake of the backslidden getting right with God that we act and behave in such a manner that we would not distract the backslidden from hearing the sermon that could turn their heart back to God. Every person needs to be sure that they behave in a manner that God would want them to act in church. So how should we act in church?

1. Come expecting something from God.

You should come to church expecting God to speak to your heart. Never just come to church just to fill your "spiritual" time with God

173

for the week. Church should be more than just a time clock to say that you've done your religious obligation for the week. It should be a time when you come desiring God to do something for you and to speak to you. If you come to church expecting to get nothing from God, you are sure to get what you came to get. However, if you come to church expecting God to speak to your heart, you will certainly find that God will speak to you during the preaching time of church.

2. Come dressed right for church.

The way you dress certainly does dictate how you act in church. I know we live in times when people think that church dress does not matter anymore, but I believe it does matter. The way you dress does dictate the way that you will act. If you dress casually when you come to church, you will act casually when you come to church.

174

We dress up for events that we believe are special. What event should be more special than going to church? Why in the world are we dressing down when we come to church? My friend, I believe you ought to dress in such a manner that if God walked inside of your church that you would not be ashamed if He saw how you were dressed. Can I remind you, He does see how you are dressed. I do not believe that we should come to church dressed in blue jeans or indecently. I believe men ought to come to church dressed in a shirt and tie, and ladies ought to come to church in dresses. I believe the way that you dress shows your heart of what you feel about God. The higher you hold God in respect, the better you will dress when you come to church.

3. Don't make church a playground.

Too many people come to church to play when they ought to come to church and ask

God to do something in their heart. If we make church a playground, we will not take the singing and the preaching of the Word of God seriously. Every parent should make sure their children are sitting in church and listening. Every teenager should make sure they're not running around in the hallways and acting like they are walking in the streets. Every child should be sure to act in such a manner that it is respectful to God if He were speaking to them. The church is not a playground it is a church. When you treat it as a playground, you will certainly not get as much from God as you could.

4. Don't use church as a place to discuss sin.

I believe one of the greatest mistakes that happens in churches are people become too familiar with each other so that they begin to talk in ways they should not talk. God says in 1 Thessalonians 5:22, *"Abstain from all appearance of evil."* God also says in Ephesians

176

4:29, *"Let no corrupt communication proceed out of your mouth, but that which is good to the use of edifying, that it may minister grace unto the hearers."* God's people should not talk about sins that they have done or are doing. God's people should not curse or swear on the church property. I'll even go as far to say that God's people should not gossip about other people when they come to church. Church is certainly not the place to gossip, nor is any place a place to gossip. There is nothing that will ruin the spirit of a church more than people discussing their sin, talking about others, talking bad about the pastor, or talking about their disagreements with God. Be sure to speak in such a manner that every word that proceeds from your mouth is a word that would encourage others to do right.

5. Sit up front.

Every person should desire to sit up front. Where you sit does determine how much you want to get from the preaching of God's Word. I have a question for you, why is it that many people will do everything they can to get to the front seats of a ball game or a rock concert but when they come to church they always want to sit in the back seat? I believe if your heart is right with God, you will desire to be as close to the front as you can.

6. Be involved.

The best way to act in church is to get involved in everything that is going on. Get involved in the preaching time by saying "Amen" or by nodding your head. Get involved by singing with all the congregational singing. Get involved in the invitation time by responding to the invitation call. The more involved you are in the church service, the more you will get from God to encourage your heart and to help you in your walk with the LORD.

7. Don't let distractions distract you.

One of the things that you will have to deal with in a church service are distractions. You must be careful that you don't let the distractions distract you from what God is wanting to give you. Let me encourage you to stay focused on the singing and the preaching of the Word of God. Turn your phone off when you go to church because it can become a great distraction to you as God is trying to give a needed truth to you. My advice is to leave anything home that would cause you to be distracted from what God wants to give you from his Word. I believe it would be good to make sure your Bible is not cluttered with a bunch of notes. I believe it is wise to make sure you leave your cell phone at home so that it doesn't tempt you to look at it during the church service. I believe it is good for you to sit up front because that way you won't see all the distractions of people moving around.

Whatever you have to do to keep from being a distraction or becoming distracted you must determine to do.

8. Respond in the preaching.

I often tell people that we don't go to church just to hear the preacher preach, but we go to church so we can respond with the preacher while he preaches. If you want to get the most out of your time at church, you would be wise to be responsive during the preaching time. For instance, when the preacher says something funny, be sure to laugh. When the preacher says something good, be sure to give a good hearty "Amen." When the preacher brings it down to the invitation time, be sure to respond accordingly to how the preacher asks you to respond. Don't come to church just to sit and watch, but come to church to be involved and respond to whatever God speaks to your heart about.

9. Respond in the invitation.

We come to church so that we can respond and make decisions. Your pastor most likely prepares and preaches his sermons so that people will make a decision. So how do we make a decision? We make a decision by responding in the invitation time. I tell people all the time that you are responding to every sermon. If you don't respond to the altar call, you've made the decision not to listen. If you respond by going to the altar to pray, you have made a decision that you want God to do something inside of your life.

There are a few reasons why you should use the altar. Use the altar because God spoke to your heart. Use the altar because you need to get something right. Use the altar because God reminded you of something that you need to keep fresh inside of your life. Use the altar to commit your burdens to the LORD.

Use the altar to find out why God did not speak to your heart during the preaching time.

Acting right in church is not something that should be looked down upon, nor should it be something that we are passive about. Acting right in church should be something that we do to make sure that we get the most from what God wants us to get at church. Let me encourage you that whenever you go to church, go to church to let God speak to your heart and to be a blessing to someone else. If you go to church for these reasons, I promise you that you will act right in church.

CHAPTER NINETEEN

PURITY

Your desire in life should be that you live your life in such a manner that you walk down the aisle the day you get married as a virgin. Sadly, we live in times when being a virgin is a rare and almost looked down upon. When a person is a virgin many think there's something wrong with you, but the fact that you are a virgin only reveals that you are a person of character. You must understand that the first person you date may not, and probably won't become the person you marry. Therefore, you are cheating your future spouse of something that belongs to them.

Despite how immoral our society is today, I still believe that a young person can still be a virgin. You have a choice to be a virgin. You have a choice to obey God and do what is right instead of living an immoral life and thinking that it won't affect you.

Often when I talk to teenagers, they look at me as if I didn't have the same temptations when I grew up that they have. Let me assure you, every generation has had to deal with the temptation of losing their purity. However, even though we live in an impure society where it is not popular to be a virgin until marriage, that doesn't change God's plan to be a virgin until marriage.

Let me teach you some Scriptural thoughts about the importance of staying pure?

1. Being a virgin is not a dirty word.

Matthew 1:23 says, *"Behold, a virgin shall be with child, and shall bring forth a son, and they shall call his name Emmanuel, which being interpreted is, God with us."* If it was right for Mary to be a virgin, it is right for you to be a virgin. If God makes an emphasis on Mary's virginity, I am sure that God is still is interested in young people being a virgin today. Being a virgin has nothing to do with what generation you live in, it has everything to do with you living for God and doing what the Scriptures teach.

2. Being a virgin is for men as well as it is for women.

Revelation 14:4 says, *"These are they which were not defiled with women; for they are virgins. These are they which follow the Lamb whithersoever he goeth. These were redeemed from among men, being the firstfruits unto God and to the Lamb."* Notice that God is talking to a group of people who were virgins. This group of men is who God was talking about.

Luke 1:27 says, *"To a virgin espoused to a man whose name was Joseph, of the house of*

David; and the virgin's name was Mary." Just like Mary was a virgin, so was Joseph. Yes it is right for a young lady to be a virgin, but it is also right for a man to be a virgin. Why was it troubling to Joseph about Mary being pregnant? The reason it troubled him is because he kept himself pure. We must understand that it does not matter what we are doing and whether we are male or female, you are to stay a virgin until you get married.

3. You can always lose your purity, but you can't always be a virgin.

2 Samuel 13:18 says, *"And she had a garment of divers colours upon her: for with such robes were the king's daughters that were virgins apparelled. Then his servant brought her out, and bolted the door after her."* This is the story about David's daughter who had been mistreated by her brother. The sad part about this story is that she lost her virginity because of a wicked brother. Let me

186

just say that any day of the week you can lose your virginity, but not any day of the week can you get it back once you've lost it. It takes more character to keep your purity than it does to lose it. In fact, it takes no character to lose your purity, but it takes great character to keep it. I am saying that God wants you to stay pure, and the fact that you can stay pure shows that you are stronger than the young people who've already lost their virginity.

4. It is God's will to be a virgin.

1 Corinthians 7:37 says, *"Nevertheless he that standeth stedfast in his heart, having no necessity, but hath power over his own will, and hath so decreed in his heart that he will keep his virgin, doeth well."* Notice that God makes it very clear that keeping your purity is staying and declaring that you're going to control your own will. How you control your will determines whether you keep your virginity. If it is God's will for someone to keep

187

their purity yesteryear, it is still God's will today.

5. Your purity is your name.

Proverbs 22:1 says, *"A good name is rather to be chosen than great riches, and loving favour rather than silver and gold."* My friend, you only have one chance to build a good name. Once you lose that good name, it is very hard to get it back. The one area you never want to lose your name in is in the area of your character or purity. When people know you to be an impure person is the day that you lose your credibility ability to be able to minister to people as you could. Keep your purity if you want to keep your name.

6. Your purity belongs to one person.

2 Corinthians 11:2 says, *"For I am jealous over you with godly jealousy: for I have espoused you to one husband, that I may*

present you as a chaste virgin to Christ." This verse is talking about the church being kept for Jesus Christ. You will notice that God wanted the church to keep itself only for Him. The reason God chose this is because this is His will for young people with each other. Your purity belongs to the person you are going to marry. To lose it with people that you'll never marry only creates heartache and trouble down the road. You owe it to the person that you are going to marry someday to keep yourself for them, and you owe it to God to keep yourself pure for Him.

7. Staying pure exemplifies your ability to have self-control.

1 Corinthians 7:37 says, *"Nevertheless he that standeth stedfast in his heart, having no necessity, but hath power over his own will, and hath so decreed in his heart that he will keep his virgin, doeth well."* You will notice that God makes a big deal about having

power over your will to keep your purity. God wants His children to have power over their will. You cannot keep your purity if you don't have the character to have power over your own will. Let me also say, if you don't have the power to keep your purity when you are single, you'll likely have the same problem once you get married. If you don't want to be immoral after you get married, don't be immoral before you get married.

8. Being pure removes possible pitfalls for your future marriage.

Deuteronomy 22:13-15 says, *"If any man take a wife, and go in unto her, and hate her, And give occasions of speech against her, and bring up an evil name upon her, and say, I took this woman, and when I came to her, I found her not a maid: Then shall the father of the damsel, and her mother, take and bring forth the tokens of the damsel's virginity unto the elders of the city in the gate:"* One of the

190

problems that many people will face in a marriage is someone with whom they had a previous relationship. If you don't want to struggle with this in your marriage, you would be wise to stay pure. The Devil will fight your marriage in more than one area; however, you can remove one weapon by staying pure.

9. It gets taken as an occasion to accuse you.

Deuteronomy 22:17 says, *"And, lo, he hath given occasions of speech against her, saying, I found not thy daughter a maid; and yet these are the tokens of my daughter's virginity. And they shall spread the cloth before the elders of the city."* Notice that this young girl was accused of being immoral, and it gave the enemy an occasion to speak against her. In Revelation 12:10 it says, *"And I heard a loud voice saying in heaven, Now is come salvation, and strength, and the kingdom of our God, and the power of his Christ: for the accuser of* our brethren *is cast down, which accused them before our God day and night."* Please understand that everything you do is a weapon that Satan will use against you, or it is a weapon that you take out of his hand. By staying pure, you remove a weapon that he will use against your conscience to keep you from serving God. If you want to be able to serve God with a clear conscience, keep your purity so that Satan cannot use your immorality as a weapon against you in the future.

10. Being pure holds a special place in God's heart.

Revelation 14:4 says, *"These are they which were not defiled with women; for they are virgins. These are they which follow the Lamb whithersoever he goeth. These were redeemed from among men, being the firstfruits unto God and to the Lamb."* God has a special place for those who keep their virginity all the way to death. I am not promoting that you stay single for the rest of your life, but I am promoting that you stay a virgin until the day you get married. If God holds a special place in Heaven for those who are virgins, this means it is God's will for you to be a virgin until you get married.

Staying pure is God's will. Staying pure is still the right thing to do. If you want to avoid the heartache that comes with losing your purity, the best thing you can do is to stay pure until the day you get married.

CHAPTER TWENTY

SOUL WINNING

Soul winning is the act of taking the Gospel to the lost world and giving them a chance to be saved. Soul winning is one of the first acts that many people performed in the Scriptures. After Jesus was tempted of the Devil, He came down the mountain and the first place He went was to the seashore where He found Andrew and led him to Himself. After Andrew got saved, the first thing he did was to bring Jesus to his brother Simon Peter and shared the Gospel with him. The first thing that Saul, who we know as the Apostle Paul, did after he got saved was to go soul winning. It says about Saul in Acts 9:20, *"And straightway he preached Christ in the synagogues, that he is the Son of God."* It is a common theme throughout the New Testament for those who get saved to immediately go and tell someone how to be saved.

Matthew 28:19 says, *"Go ye therefore, and teach all nations, baptizing them in the name of the Father, and of the Son, and of the Holy Ghost:"* This command is reiterated in Acts 1:8 where it says, *"But ye shall receive power, after that the Holy Ghost is come upon you: and ye shall be witnesses unto me both in Jerusalem, and in all Judaea, and in Samaria, and unto the uttermost part of the earth."*

You will notice in both of these verses the importance of going and witnessing. Soul winning is the way that the believer goes and shares the Gospel with the lost. Let me first share what soul winning is not.

1. Soul winning is not having service groups that go out into the community to help people.

I am not against going and helping other people; however, Jesus never went into the community in a service group to help people

195

around their homes. Jesus went directly from person-to-person and shared the Gospel.

2. Soul winning is not just passing out tracts.

I am not against passing out tracts because a tract should have the Gospel on it; however, many believers want to just pass out tracts and never tell anyone how to be saved. God's command to the believer is to witness about Christ. Though there is a place for passing out Gospel tracts, it would be good to go beyond just giving a tract and also share the Gospel with the one to whom you gave the tract.

3. Soul winning is not a lifestyle.

It's certainly much easier to tell others about Christ if you are living the Christian life, but people won't get saved just because you live a good life. Jesus, the perfect Son of God, certainly lived a good life, but He shared the

Gospel to give an example of the importance of witnessing to others about Christ.

4. Soul winning is not done to build a church or ministry.

Many people think they should go soul winning to build their church. Soul winning certainly can contribute to the growth of the church, but you don't go soul winning to build the church; you go soul winning to reach the lost for Christ. If you go soul winning to build the church, when your church doesn't grow, you will stop going soul winning. The purpose of soul winning is to give the Gospel to the lost so they have an opportunity to get saved.

WHY GO SOUL WINNING?

1. Because God commands you to go soul winning.

If nobody got saved, you are still to be a soul winner. If soul winning doesn't build the church, you are still to tell others about Christ. One purpose of going soul winning is so that you can be obedient to Christ's command to tell others about Him.

2. Soul winning is the decent thing to do.

There is nothing more decent for the believer than to tell others how they settled their eternity. It is decent because you have the answer to keep others from going to Hell. If you know how to keep others from going to Hell, it is the decent thing to do to tell them what they can do to settle their eternity for Heaven.

3. Soul winning is the selfless thing to do.

Going soul winning has nothing to do about you, but everything to do about others. Being a soul winner is one of the most selfless things a believer can do. You can't be selfish and be a soul winner at the same time.

4. Soul winning shows your appreciation for what God has done for you.

The best way you could show God that you love Him and appreciate what He did to save you from Hell is to tell everyone the Gospel with whom you come in contact. Going soul winning is one way of telling God "thank you" for saving your soul from Hell.

5. Soul winning is the only way to save your nation.

There are many things you can do that are good to help your nation, but there is only one thing you can do to change the heart of people that will save your nation, and that one thing is to reach them with the Gospel. The more people you reach with the Gospel, the more the Holy Spirit has the opportunity to change the heart of those individuals. The more individuals whose heart is changed with the Gospel, the more your nation will change for the good.

6. Soul winning is the only way to reach a soul.

Lost people will not hear the Gospel without the believer going and telling them how to be saved. The Book of Acts is filled with the early believers telling people daily how to be saved. You should be a soul winner because most people will never hear the Gospel without someone telling them.

Because it is the right thing to be a soul winner, let me share what it will take for you to be a faithful soul winner.

1. You will never go soul winning if you don't have a time to go.

The best way to be faithful to soul winning is to set a time every week to go. Of course, you should always be on the lookout for souls, but you must have a set time that you keep weekly if you are going to be faithful as a soul winner.

2. Soul winning is not about your abilities, it's about the power of the Gospel.

Don't let your insecurity keep you from being a soul winner. Many believers won't go because they are afraid they will mess up. As long as you tell the Gospel, the Gospel will do its work in the heart of the lost. People don't get saved because of your abilities, but they get saved because of the power of the Gospel. The Gospel given, no matter how good the delivery was, is what does the work to convict the lost and save the sinner.

3. Soul winning takes faith that God can use you to do it.

One of the great benefits of soul winning is that it will increase your faith. It takes faith to be a soul winner; therefore, every time you share the Gospel, you are increasing your faith, which pleases God.

4. If you are going to be a soul winner, you must GO.

The first word in the Great Commission is *"Go."* People will never be saved without you going. The best time to go is now. The best place to go is anywhere. The best person to give the Gospel to is the first person you see. My friend, you will never be a soul winner until you go. Let me challenge you to go and be a soul winner and live a life of leading people to Christ. It is the most rewarding act God allows us to do that brings joy to your Christian walk.

CHAPTER TWENTY-ONE

WALK WITH GOD

One of my favorite times every day is when I wake up, because that is the time I take daily to walk with God in the Scriptures and pray. I know that the thought of reading the Scriptures daily and spending time in prayer does not sound exciting, but if you are going to successfully enjoy serving God for the rest of your life, you will have to learn to walk with God daily. This chapter is not to show you how to walk with God in the Scriptures and prayer, but why you are supposed to do it. Let me explain why you should walk with God daily.

WHY DO WE WALK WITH GOD?

1. Because God commands it.

Joshua 1:8 says, *"This book of the law shall not depart out of thy mouth; but thou shalt meditate therein day and night, that thou mayest observe to do according to all that is written therein: for then thou shalt make thy way prosperous, and then thou shalt have good success."* You cannot meditate in something that you don't read. You have to know what something says before you can spend time meditating or thinking about it.

God commands the believer in John 5:39 to *"Search the scriptures..."* One of the best mindsets you must have as you go to read God's Word is not that you are doing it because you have to, but you are doing it because you are digging for buried treasures that God wants you to find so that they can help you to better your life.

2. Because you agree with God.

Amos 3:3 says, *"Can two walk together, except they be agreed?"* If you are right with God, you will want to walk with Him in His Word. In fact, whether you read God's Word and pray daily reveals whether your heart is right with God.

3. Because walking with God gives you God's wisdom.

Everybody needs wisdom on a daily basis. You don't just need wisdom, but you need godly wisdom to help you look at your daily decisions through the eyes of God. There is no better place to find this wisdom other than in God's Word. Proverbs 2:6 says, *"For the LORD giveth wisdom: out of his mouth cometh knowledge and understanding."* God's Word is an endless source of wisdom to help you in any decision you need to make. You walk with God so you can glean wisdom from His Word.

4. Because walking with God spiritually feeds you.

Anything that is going to grow is going to need spiritual nourishment. You are supposed to grow as a believer, but you cannot grow unless you get the spiritual nourishment from God's Word. Jesus said in Matthew 4:4, *"...It is written, Man shall not live by bread alone, but by every word that proceedeth out of the mouth of God."* You will notice that God's Word will not only feed you, but it will satisfy your daily hunger to be with God.

5. Because walking with God makes you more like God.

When you are right with God, you will have a heart that desires to be more like Him. This will only be accomplished by spending time with Him in His Word, and walking with Him daily in prayer. Proverbs 13:20 says, *"He that walketh with wise men shall be wise..."* If walking with wise men will make a person wise, so, walking with God will make you more like Him. If the only reason you choose to read the Scriptures daily and walk with God in prayer is to be more like God, that in itself is a good reason to walk with God.

6. Because walking with God will give you the mind of Christ.

The believer needs the mind of Christ for everything they do for Him. You don't need your mind to do God's work, but you need His mind to do it. Philippians 2:5 says, *"Let this mind be in you, which was also in Christ Jesus:"* There is no better place to find out the mind of God, His philosophy, and His methods of doing things other than in God's Word.

7. Because walking with God will keep you from sin.

There is an old saying, "Sin will keep you from this Book, but this Book will keep you from sin." The book being talked about is God's Word. Psalm 119:11 says, *"Thy word have I hid in mine heart, that I might not sin against thee."* You will find it much easier to fight sin if you are hiding God's Word in your mind. How do you hide God's Word in your mind? You hide it there by reading His Word regularly and by memorizing it.

8. Because walking with God will convict you of sin.

You cannot read God's Word without it convicting you of any sin in your life. Hebrews 4:12 says, *"For the word of God is quick, and powerful, and sharper than any twoedged sword, piercing even to the dividing asunder of soul and spirit, and of the joints and marrow, and is a discerner of the thoughts and intents of the heart."* God's Word has a way of piercing through the walls that you have placed up to try to hide your sin. People talk about believers hiding their sin, and they do, but God's Word has a way of shining His light and exposing your conscience, forcing you to make a decision about it. If you don't want sin

208

to ruin your life, reading God's Word daily will help you to avoid it.

9. Because walking with God will protect your mind.

Ephesians 6:17 says, *"And take the helmet of salvation, and the sword of the Spirit, which is the word of God:"* God's Word is the helmet that protects your mind from thinking things it should not think. If you have problems with having the wrong thoughts, you must fill your mind with God's Word because it will cleanse your mind of those thoughts. Not only will it cleanse your mind of sin, but it will help you to fortify your mind so that the wrong thoughts won't come back.

10. Because walking with God will increase your faith.

One of the big reasons I enjoy reading God's Word is because it challenges my faith.

Every time I read the stories of faith in the Scriptures, it challenges me to do more for God by faith. This should not surprise you that God's Word will challenge and increase your faith. Romans 10:17 says, *"So then faith cometh by hearing, and hearing by the word of God."* You will find that God's Word is like a spiritual steroid to your faith and will cause it to grow because His Word will challenge you to do more for Him.

11. Because walking with God will show you God's will for your life.

The great desire of every believer should be to find the purpose for why God placed them on this Earth, and that purpose would be His will for your life. God's Word is the only place that will help you to find His will. Psalm 119:105 says, *"Thy word is a lamp unto my feet, and a light unto my path."* It is God's Word that opens your mind to God's mind, and it is when you have God's mind that you will know what His will is for your life.

My friend, you will never regret spending time with God. Walking with God should never be a drudgery or an action of requirement, though God does command it; it should be something that you look forward to because of all the benefits that walking with God will do for you.

CHAPTER TWENTY-TWO

OBEYING AND HONORING YOUR PARENTS

I grew up in a home where obeying and honoring my parents was not a choice; it was expected. Sadly, it seems like the days where parents commanded respect are days of the past. However, God's Word does not change about the command to obey and honor your parents. Ephesians 6:1-2 says, *"Children, obey your parents in the Lord: for this is right. Honour thy father and mother; (which is the first commandment with promise;)"*

You will notice that this was not a suggestion to obey your parents and to honor them, but it was a command. God feels so adamantly about children obeying their parents that He promised a blessing to those children who obey, and a deadly consequence to those who did not. The blessing is found in Ephesians 6:3 which says, *"That it may be well with thee, and thou mayest live long on the earth."* To promise long life is quite the promise that God gives to anyone who chooses to obey and honor their parents.

On the other hand, God commands that a child be disciplined if they didn't obey their parents. In Deuteronomy 21:18-21, God told the Israelites that the child who rebelled and wouldn't listen to their parents was to be stoned to death. It doesn't matter if we agree with God's punishment or not; one thing that is clear is that God expects children to obey and honor their parents. Let me show you why the Scriptures are clear about you obeying and honoring your parents.

1. Your parents are your authority.

God expects every believer to obey their authority. Hebrews 13:17 says, *"Obey them that have the rule over you, and submit yourselves..."* According to Ephesians 6:1-2, your parents are the authorities who have the rule over you. Because your parents are your authority, you are to obey and honor them.

2. It is the right thing to do to obey and honor your parents.

It is the right thing to obey and honor your parents because they are the ones who pay your bills. A child doesn't pay the mortgage, purchase the groceries, or care for the daily life provision, but the parents are the ones who pay for you to enjoy the comforts of life. The fact that they are paying the bills should cause you to want to obey and honor your parents.

3. Your obedience and honor of your parents shows your respect for God.

Your parents are the in-between between you and God. How you obey your parents shows your heart and how well you obey God. You show me a child who is rebellious towards their parents, and I will show you a child who is rebellious towards God. You can't be right with God and not be right with your parents.

4. **God didn't say your parents had to be good parents for you to honor and obey them.**

God's command to obey was not dependent upon how good they are, but His command was based on the fact that He expects you to obey them. Your parents may not be the best parents in the world, but they are still your parents and God expects you to obey them. God didn't say, "Obey your parent in the Lord when they are good parents." God did say that you are to obey them no matter how good or bad you think they are. It doesn't matter that your parents may not be doing what they are supposed to be doing, but it does matter that you are supposed to do what God commands you to do, and that is to obey and honor your parents.

215

5. **God holds you accountable for how you obey and honor your parents, and not how your parents treat you.**

God's accountability for the child is to obey. You will notice in Ephesians 6:4 God says, *"And, ye fathers, provoke not your children to wrath…"* What this verse is showing is that God holds the parents accountable for how they parent you, but He holds you accountable for how well you obey them no matter how they treat you.

6. **If for any reason you obey or honor your parents, obey and honor them for the LORD.**

Notice what Ephesians 6:1 says, *"Children, obey your parents in the Lord…"* In other words, God is saying that if the only reason you obey them is so that you can be right with Him, then obey them for the Lord's sake. When your parents are not what they are supposed

216

to be, you still have a reason to be obedient to them and that reason is that you are doing it for the LORD's sake; therefore, you always have a reason to obey your parents because the LORD has always been good to you.

7. Obeying and honoring your parents gives a promise to live a longer life.

I don't know about you, but I do want to live a longer life. I don't want my life cut short because I didn't obey my parents. The promise of long life is found in Ephesians 6:3 which says, *"That it may be well with thee, and thou mayest live long on the earth."* If you don't want your life cut short, you would be wise to obey your parents. Why? Because they look out for your well-being. Many of the things they tell you to do is to keep you safe and from harm in the future. Even if your parents are not the best parents, what they tell you to do is for your benefit and will help you to live a longer life.

8. **Obeying and honoring your parents gives a promise that God will deal well with you.**

You should desire to be in God's favor. Being in God's favor means that you have a better chance of getting God to answer your prayers and to bless you. God's promise to the child who obeys is that He will *"be well with thee."* Don't you want God to be good to you all the time? If you do, you should obey God's command to obey and honor your parents.

9. **How you obey and honor your parents will dictate how you treat others.**

Your treatment of your parents always comes out in how you treat others. Why? Because how you treat your parents shows how much respect you have for others. If you don't have enough respect to treat your parents properly enough to obey them, you certainly won't have any respect to treat other people and authorities the right way.

My friend, it may not be popular to obey and honor your parent, but it is still the right thing to do. It may not be easy to obey and honor your parents, but God never said to obey and honor them when it was easy. The benefits of obeying and honoring your parents far outweighs the satisfaction of doing what you want to do. It may be tempting to do your own thing, but it is the right thing to do to obey and honor your parents.

CHAPTER TWENTY-THREE

RESPECTING AUTHORITIES

Respect is treating people with dignity and honor. Philippians 2:3 says, *"Let nothing be done through strife or vainglory; but in lowliness of mind let each esteem other better than themselves."* God's model for respect is found in the phrase, *"...let each esteem other better than themselves."* In other words, treat others with the respect that you would want them to treat you is the best way to get respect.

You should respect others because you never know who you are talking to and how they will influence your future. It is best to treat everybody as if they were your future boss. There are numerous stories of people who were kind to someone they did not know who eventually became someone who helped them financially or someone from whom they wanted a job. It is not only Scriptural to respect authorities, but it is vital to your future. Let me give you a few thoughts that will help you as to why you should respect authorities.

1. You should respect everyone because you are no better than anyone.

To treat one person differently from another is not only unwise, but it is also unscriptural. To esteem others better than yourself is not a suggestion but a command. To disrespect people is to say that you are better than them, which is arrogant and wrong. You are not better than anyone; therefore, you should treat everyone with respect. Leaders must be careful to treat those you lead with respect, even those who you don't like.

2. You are no less than anyone.

Just as you are not better than others, you are also not any less than others. The command to esteem others better than yourself is not saying that you are inferior, but that you are equal to everyone else. It is just as wrong to think of yourself as inferior to another as it is to believe that you are better than another. You are no better or worse than any other person. This is why you should respect ALL people.

3. Respect has everything to do with living together.

At the end of the day, we all live in the same world. Imagine how much better this world would be if we treated everyone with the same respect that we would want them to treat us. You are not making the world you live in better by disrespecting others. How you treat others eventually comes back to how others will treat you. If Jesus honored and respected everyone He came into contact with, so you should also respect everyone.

4. How you treat authorities shows your respect for God.

Romans 13:1-2 says, *"Let every soul be subject unto the higher powers. For there is no power but of God: the powers that be are ordained of God. Whosoever therefore resisteth the power, resisteth the ordinance of God..."* Notice that God says that there is *"no power but of God."* He is saying that He has ordained the office of authority, and it doesn't matter who holds that office; you should be subject to them, which would also include respecting them. Your respect for authority reveals what you feel about God.

5. Your respect for authority reveals your respect for your fellow citizen.

When you don't respect the authorities who are in power to protect everyone's freedom, you are showing disrespect for your fellow citizen who your disrespect affects. You will find that when you don't respect God, you won't respect authorities, which results in not respecting your fellow citizen.

6. Your respect for your fellow citizen shows how much you respect yourself.

The biggest reason people have a problem with respecting others is because they don't respect themselves. The disrespect of yourself always leaks out into disrespecting others. How can you respect others when you don't respect yourself enough to do what the Scriptures teach? The fact is, you can't!

7. How you respect others will show in how you respect the properties of others.

Another area that needs improvement with people is by respecting another's property. You have no right to touch another's property without their permission. One of the reasons we see people breaking into businesses in riots is because they have no respect for others or for another's property. If you don't want someone to mistreat your personal property, don't disrespect their property.

8. Respecting authority has to do with respecting the position more than the person.

When I talk about respecting authority, I am mainly trying to get you to realize that you should respect the office. You don't have to like the person of authority to respect the position of authority. For instance, you don't have to like the police officer, but you should respect him or her because of their position. This can apply to your school teacher, Sunday school teacher, bus captain, or pastor. In all of these areas, you should treat them with great respect because their position deserves respect. I believe you should address them properly, talk to them properly, never curse at them, and treat them in the manner that you would treat God if He were the one who was physically holding that position.

9. How you respect authority often determines how people will respect you.

My friend, if you want others to treat you with respect, you had better learn to treat them with respect. Just because they might not treat you with respect doesn't take away your responsibility to treat them with respect. You may have a few who treat you with disrespect, but you will find that most people will treat you to the same degree that you respect others.

The Scriptures are clear that we are to respect each other. If you want to be in favor with God, you should treat everyone with respect.

Made in the USA
Columbia, SC
28 May 2022

61040091R00126